SINS OF MY MOTHER

By

Terri Jones Salter

xulon
PRESS

Copyright © 2004 by Terri Jones Salter

Sins of My Mother
by Terri Jones Salter

Printed in the United States of America

ISBN 1-594672-98-9

Unless otherwise indicated, Bible quotations are taken from the King James Version.

www.xulonpress.com

DEDICATION

This book is dedicated to my mother, Minister Lynda Joyce Jones (1954-1999)- a woman of great integrity and character. She taught me that a mother is a teacher, a counselor, and a role model. Only after fulfilling those roles well, does she later become a most cherished friend. I will praise the Lord forever for lending you to me, even if it was…just for a season.

ACKNOWLEDGEMENTS

I'd like to thank my hero, my husband, De'Andre M. Salter for believing in me when I didn't even believe in myself. Thank you for your undying support. I'm eternally grateful.

I'd also like to thank my pastor, Pastor Emma Salter and my family, who truly believe anything I write is worth reading. A special thanks to my sister, Sherri, for babysitting my little ones as I completed this book.

EXODUS 20:3-5

"Thou shalt have no other Gods before Me. Thou shalt not make unto thee any graven images or any likeness of anything that is in Heaven above or that is in the earth beneath or that is in the water under the earth: Thou shalt not bow down thyself to them nor serve them for I the LORD, thy God, am a jealous God, _visiting the iniquity of the fathers upon the children unto the third and fourth generation of them that hate Me_.

CHAPTER 1

UNPLANNED PARENTHOOD

Her name was Billie Jean. Not the one Michael Jackson sang about although she could have been. After all, she was always guessing as to who the father of her children might be…all except two, me and my sister. She knew who our father was; the only man she ever truly loved or truly wanted and we were the only children whose conception she had planned. During childhood, we were always reminded of that, as she called out, "I loved your father, but he was a no good liar. He didn't love me. He just walked out and left me with twins. He didn't love ya'll either!"

Hmm, I wondered, did he really not love us or did he tell us he was going to the store and never come back because she drove him away. The latter seemed more believable. Don't get me wrong, Billie (as she made all her children call her because she said she was too young to be anybody's mama) wasn't all that bad as a mother in the beginning. She read me bedtime stories when I was small. She sang songs to me. She was actually happy once and in turn she made us happy but after my father left she fell into a severe depression. Billie even had to be committed for a little while and we were sent to live with our grandparents.

To this day I still say they are the reason why I'm sane now. After Billie got out of the hospital she began to drink, I guess to ease the pain. First, she drank at night to help her battle the insomnia that resulted from the ache of which she could not rid herself. Then she drank in the morning to give herself reason to make it through another day. Finally, she became a drunk. I knew it and everyone in the projects knew it...but, Billie? No, she said she was finally thinking of herself. After all, she was just a kid and she wanted to have fun. She was only eighteen going on nineteen. It wasn't her fault some no good man had stolen her heart, knocked her up, married her and abandoned her with twins. It wasn't her fault and she should not have to bear punishment. Shoot, Rosa and I were almost four anyway. We knew how to tie our shoes, how to use the bathroom by ourselves and how to dress ourselves. We didn't need her around all the time. Once Billie had justified her neglect in her own mind, then came the parties. Our apartment became party central for all of the drunks in the neighborhood. It also became a home away from home for everybody else's husband. It seemed like men came in and out of the house constantly. Tall ones, short ones, dark ones, light ones...all somebody else's one. My grandparents got so fed up with Billie's rendezvous and her constant drunkenness that they took my sister and I in. They told Billie that she would never see us again until she straightened up. To my surprise, Billie fought my grandfather as he packed our things. She cried as grandma took our little hands and pulled us out the door. She ran behind the car as it pulled off. I got on my knees in the back seat and as I looked out the window, I could see her sitting in the middle of the street crying. Crying, like she did that time when she got the call from Alabama informing her that her mother had died. She was weeping, like she had when three days had passed with us sitting next to the window day and night, even eating there, waiting for my daddy to come home. Then, after the ninth day with no sight of him and no phone call, knowing he was never coming back. Looking at my mother in the middle of the street, I realized, for the first time, that she loved us. We hadn't been gone five months when Billie called one day in one of her drunken stupors, telling me to get Rosa and for us both to get on the phone. We could hear the cars whiz by as she spoke. Billie's phone had been cut off so she was obviously calling from a pay phone. She told us she wasn't going to drink anymore and that she missed us. Then she began to cry and asked to speak to Grandma Helen and Grandpa George. So they came to the phone. All we could hear was shouting and screaming. "What's wrong with you," I heard grandma yell, "Well, don't expect us to bail you out of this one, I will not turn this house into a foster home for illegitimate kids…you're on your own and for God's sake, stop drinking!" Grandma slammed the phone down but grandpa kept talking on the other phone. He asked her if she needed money because he knew of someone who could take care of it for her. She must have said that she didn't want it taken care of because then grandpa began to beg her not to keep it. He told her that she should get herself some help so that she could take care of us. Grandpa apologized for how his son had left her, and explained how much he loved us, "But," he said, "I can not be responsible for anybody else's bastard child." Pausing for a brief moment, he hung up. Later Rosa and I had come to learn that Billie was pregnant by one of three men and seven months later Jackie was born. Billie did stop drinking while she was pregnant and grandma and grandpa even let us go visit her sometimes.

Although the drinking had ceased, parties, and even the men had not. She would parade us around like Teddy Bears at a child's tea party asking everyone to look at how big we were getting. She said we were going to be tall like our father and we were spitting images of him too. Then she'd begin to cry and tell us to go to bed. After Jackie was born, Billie took out time to be a mother. That is, to feed, to burp and to diaper. She even got a job working in a grocery store. She still drank, but she was never really drunk anymore because it took more liquor to intoxicate her. She couldn't afford to buy more since she now had a one-year-old daughter and another on the way. This pattern continued the next year as well. Billie found herself pregnant and then before Brandy was even one year old she was pregnant again. She said her most prized possessions were her children and her liquor so she named all of my sisters after her favorite drinks, with the exception of my youngest sister Dorothy, who was named after her favorite movie star, Dorothy Dandridge. Jackie was named in honor of Jack Daniels. Then there was Brandy and Gina (named after gin). Billie now had six kids, all girls and no permanent man in sight. Because she was depressed, she drank even more. She began to lose jobs because she did not allow herself to stay sober during the day. It seemed like she drank just about all day, everyday. About two years after Dorothy was born, Billie suddenly decided she would get off welfare, it seemed like she had gained new found pride, like someone had resuscitated her after years of death. She said that she had to take control of her destiny. She said she wanted to get herself together, for good this time. She wanted to be strong like the women who played such an important role in the black folks' struggle for equality. Women like Angela Davis who put their lives on the line to secure protection for their people by being a member of the Black Panther Movement. She said Rosa Parks was a hero in her own way too, refusing to give her seat up as she had done so many times before. She was tired. Didn't she have a right to sit there and rest her feet? Sure she did. Billie went on and on about how she was taking charge of her life as they had taken charge of theirs.

Rosa Parks and Angela Davis were Billie's two favorite people from the Civil Rights struggle. She said it was a breath of fresh air to see women taking their rightful place, right beside the men. That's why she named Rosa and I after them.

As I heard my grandparents talk about this sudden change in Billie, grandpa was elated, grandma was suspicious.

"What could make her do such a 180 degree turn about?"

"Prayer changes things, you know that Helen."

"Yeah, I know that, but something's telling me a man's behind this and not a miracle!"

Sure enough, grandma had been right. Billie did have a man...one man in her life. He was there when we went to visit. He was short and about Billie's complexion, very fair-skinned. He had light brown eyes and one of those process hairdos. He had a light mustache above his lip and was quite skinny. His name was Bruce. He was the manager at some department store and he was very different than our 6'3", black as the night, stout father. Everything about him was different. I remember my father always laughing, making Billie and us laugh too. Yep, that was daddy. He always had a smile on his face, always playing jokes and pranks...until right before he left. Then, he seemed to become more serious; always pondering over bills, complaining about his boss. His smiles turned into frowns and he began to isolate himself. I saw it. Billie didn't.

She still went around the house joking and laughing, only instead of seeming fun and full of excitement like dad did when he joked, she just seemed downright silly. Here the man was, obviously stressed out, carrying the burden of a man when he was just a boy and she's going around telling the same old jokes and playing the same old pranks. Daddy needed Billie to put her arms around him and tell him everything was going to be all right. He needed to know that his hard work in Mr. John's factory was appreciated. After all, he had given up an opportunity to go to college to marry Billie and work in this factory. He had loved Billie and he wanted so much to do the right thing when she told him she was pregnant. Daddy needed a woman to help him bear his burden, but it wasn't Billie's fault that he had married a little girl.

Well, anyway this Bruce guy was always so serious, at least around us he was. I don't know if he even liked kids. Don't get me wrong, he was nice. He gave Rosa and I a dime every time we came over. It's just that I don't ever remember him laughing except when all six of us lay in the bedroom; Rosa and I on the top part of the bed, Brandy and Dorothy on the bottom. Jackie and Gina lay on a mattress on the floor. Even though Rosa and I were the oldest, Billie didn't want to catch the wrath of Helen by allowing her "dear grandchildren" to sleep on the floor where there was a draft, not to even mention roaches. Unfortunately, roaches don't limit their roaming ground to the floor, so every now and then we'd have to brush one or two off of the cover.

We could hear Billie and Bruce in the other room laughing and singing. Then we'd hear Billie making weird sounds. Bruce would let out a holler, everything would be silent and I'd be left in the dark still room, looking up at the ceiling and wondering, why? Why didn't Bruce ever laugh like that when we were around?

Billie seemed so happy. The parties had ceased; the men had stopped banging on the door screaming, "Billie, let me in woman!" Even the drinking had stopped. Bruce had given her a job at the store where he worked and Billie's friend watched the girls for her during the day. Billie took out the time to pick out our clothes, feed us and even comb all of our hair. Before, she had always been too drunk to even notice if we had gone unfed or if Jackie had put a winter sweater on Brandy along with a pair of summer shorts.

As Billie stood over me parting my hair in sections and braiding it, I looked up at her. I had never really noticed how beautiful she was. Billie's father was a white man and it is my assumption that she probably looked a lot like him. Her high cheekbones, her fair skin, her thick long wavy hair, her full lips and what really struck me was her beautiful brown eyes. They were no longer red; no longer puffy...they shone brightly. They even seemed to smile, if eyes can do that. She was truly happy and so was I.

"Keep your head straight Angela," Billie yelled, "You gonna make these parts crooked and then, you gonna look like a fool. Now keep still and stop looking up, so I can do this right."

"O.K. Billie."

I knew that she wanted us to look nice and she wanted everything to be right when Bruce came over tonight. She was cooking a special meal: chicken, stuffing, collard greens, cornbread and macaroni and cheese. She had spent almost her whole check grocery shopping the day before to prepare it.

Bruce was due to arrive at 6:00. By the time 8:00 rolled around, all of us were starving.

"Billie can we eat now?" Rosa courageously inquired.

Billie just sat there, in the kitchen chair staring into space. Rosa asked again thinking perhaps Billie didn't hear her. Again, there was no response. Rosa came back in the room where we all were waiting to hear the outcome of her inquiry.

"What she say?" I asked.

Rosa said, "She hasn't said a thing, she just sat there."

We all crept around the corner and peeked to see if what Rosa had said was true. Sure enough, Billie sat there. She wasn't crying. She wasn't moaning. She just sat there. She looked at all of us, motioned for us to sit down, fixed our plates and left the room. I helped Dorothy by slicing and mushing her food with her fork. After we all ate, they went into the room. I stood on a chair and washed our dishes. Once I was finished, I took a deep breath and started for Billie's room. This is my chance, I thought. I can hug her and tell her how much I love her. I can tell her not to worry - everything's going to be all right, like daddy had wanted her to do him. I would be there for my mother like I wanted so much for her to be there for me.

I got to the room and it was empty. All that stood was Billie's unmade bed, with the thin quilted blanket that her grandmother had sent her at the bottom and her pine dresser that had drawers missing. Daddy had gotten it off of the street. He said he couldn't believe someone was going to throw it away. In the middle of the floor lay that small blue prickly rug that I hated so much. I remember when Billie bought that thing. Daddy had been so upset. He said he couldn't believe Billie would go waste money on something we didn't need, especially when he was struggling so hard just to keep a roof over our heads and food in our mouths. Billie had claimed she did need it because at night her feet got cold when she got out of the bed to get something. It had been fluffy then. Now here it was matted and prickly because she had washed it so often. The bed, the dresser, the rug, but no Billie. Where was Billie? I walked through the big room that Billie called the living room; one small tattered sofa and a black and white t.v. sitting on top of a crate. Wrinkled sheets were tacked up to the window. I remember Billie saying she was going to buy blinds now that she was working.

I went into the kitchen again and then I looked in the room where my sisters were. Brandy and Jackie were playing tic tac toe. Rosa was coloring by herself in the corner and the others were scattered about the room playing with headless dolls and blocks, but there was no Billie. I checked the bathroom. She wasn't there either. I had not heard the door shut so how could she have left? It seemed like hours passed before I heard a knock at the door. Everyone had gone to sleep but me, I was worried sick. Why had Billie left us in the apartment by ourselves? We were only children; nine years old, five, four, three and two. As I walked to the front door, I looked at the clock hanging on the living room wall, it was midnight. I climbed onto a chair, put the chain on the door and opened it slightly. It was Bruce.

"Hi Angela. Tell your mommy I'm here," he said.

Mommy? I thought, you mean Billie? But I said, "Billie's not here right now."

"She left ya'll in there by yourselves? Where did she go?"

That's a very good question, I thought. "I don't know," I said.

Bruce told me to let him in. He said that he wanted to explain to Billie why he had not been able to make it to dinner. Now, my grandparents told me never to open doors for strangers, never to talk to them, but Bruce was no stranger, so I let him in. He sat down on the floor. I turned on the television and we waited and we waited and waited some more. I must have been sleep when Billie came home because when I heard the screams, I opened my eyes. I could tell by her staggering movements and her slurred speech that she was drunk. And those eyes, those beautiful brown eyes were red once more. Bruce was screaming, "Who is this? Who is he, huh?" I sat up and sure enough there was some man standing in the door with a bottle of liquor wrapped in a brown bag. Billie was crying and trying to talk, but her lips just couldn't seem to figure out what her mind was trying to say. The man in the door saw Bruce approaching him, he called Billie a "slut" and ran. I looked at the clock, it was 4 a.m. Bruce grabbed Billie by the arms and shook her violently. He told her that his brother in Long Island had a heart attack. He had to leave work early to get there and he'd been with his mother and father all night. After his brother had "come out of the woods", he rushed back here. Bruce said he realized that in all the chaos, he had forgotten to call. Not that he could have anyway because Billie's phone was disconnected again. He said he knew that she was probably thinking he had stood her up. He asked her why she had left all of us in the apartment; why had she gotten drunk and why had she felt the need to be with that man?

"I thought you loved me Billie. Kids aren't really my thing, but I've been trying because I really care about you…and now as soon as my back is turned you go do this."

Bruce pushed her and Billie fell back onto the sofa. By that time, I had crawled into one of the corners. I just watched as my knees seemed to tremble. I was scared.

"You know, my mother was right. You ain't nothing but a welfare ho!"

Billie still couldn't get her words together and now Rosa, Brandy and Jackie were peeking around the corner. Bruce walked toward the door and Billie tried to stand, but she couldn't. I felt like screaming, "Stop him, stop him please!" Until that moment, I didn't know if I liked Bruce or not. Even now, I'm not sure if I ever liked him, but I do know that I liked the change he made in Billie. I liked seeing her happy. But once again, she had messed it up. In my heart, I felt like she had driven my daddy away by not picking up on what he needed and now she was driving Bruce away too.

Billie slid out of the sofa and crawled over to where Bruce was standing. She grabbed on to his ankle and finally muttered an audible word. She cried out, "Please, please" I could see Bruce's eyes turn red, almost as red as Billie's. He looked at us and then he pulled Billie's arms from around his ankle like you pull the wrapper off of a candy bar…and he left. Billie laid there sobbing because of depression and I cowered in the corner sobbing just as hard because of disgust.

I was so anxious to go back home on Sunday that I left my weekend bag at Billie's. Rosa never said a word about what we had witnessed that weekend and neither did I. I vowed to myself that I would never go back, a vow that I did not keep.

CHAPTER TWO

SCANDALOUS

I t didn't take long for things to go back to normal, with Billie drinking all of the time. She had even quit her job and went back on welfare. Bruce did come by a couple of times after that night, but things were never the same again. At night we no longer heard laughing and singing as we had heard before, just the weird noises, the holler and silence. The slamming of the front door as Bruce left would interrupt the silence. One day he slammed the door and we never saw him again. I overheard Edna, one of Billie's drunken friends telling her that he was seeing Thelma in apartment building F. Thelma had always told Billie how lucky she was to have Bruce. Now, she had him.

Edna was about the only woman in the projects more scandalous than Billie. They had become fast friends, which was unusual because Billie didn't have girlfriends. They got along great. They only argued over liquor. Billie always accused Edna of drinking some of the alcohol she kept stashed away in the apartment and then mixing that which remained in the bottle with water. Her friend always denied it, but Billie never believed her.

Edna had eight kids, but only four lived with her. Two had been taken by the state and the other two lived with their father and his wife. It seemed like the worst four are the ones she kept. If anyone had something stolen from their homes, chances are Leland, Edna's oldest son, had been over their house when it was taken. Edna said it was just coincidence, but we all knew the truth. Her kids ran around with their faces dirty and their hair unbrushed and uncombed. Edna's thirteen-year old daughter, Joy, was already sexually active and known by the fourteen-year old boys as the biggest "trick" in the projects. Chance, her middle son, got kicks out of torturing others and Thurman, her youngest, ran around spitting on people and always reeked of urine.

Yep, Edna's kids would've made Bebe's kids look like misunderstood angels. Edna always left them in the house alone while she went to go do "her thing." I have to admit though, Edna had it worst than Billie. She was not only an alcoholic, but she was a dope fiend as well. She started off pretty light, as light as drugs can get- marijuana- but then slowly graduated to the higher levels- cocaine and heroine. See, she had this man named Reggie. He was a supplier for most of the projects. He took such a liking to Edna that he began to give her free samples of coke. It didn't take long before she got hooked. She began to look really bad and believe me; no one was accustomed to seeing Edna look bad. She wasn't an ugly woman, but she wasn't pretty either. She had dark skin, big hips and legs, and a small waistline. She was very proud of her waist and wore a belt with everything. Edna was the only woman I've ever seen wear a belt with a housecoat. She always looked nice. She'd squeeze her big butt into some shimmering dress, slap on a wig, and go sit down at Sugar Daddy's, the local bar, nearly every night. Edna would go home with some man, whoever had the smoothest rap that night, and be seen creeping in her apartment the next day. No one was ever successful at creeping in the projects because of those loud doors. No matter how discreet you had been, BAM!! Those doors would always give you away.

After Edna hooked up with Reggie, she rarely ever went to Sugar Daddy's anymore. Once, when Billie was talking about giving up liquor in one of her drunken teary-eyed confessions, Edna told her the best way to let go of alcohol was to hold on to smack. Edna barely came around the house anymore. Sometimes when Rosa and I were visiting Billie and we'd go downstairs to play on the stoop, we'd see Edna sitting in the hallway dozing as a result of her latest high. She'd be mumbling to herself, her hair uncombed and reeking of urine as her son used to. Chance and Thurman were taken by the state. Leland was doing his own thing and it was rumored that Joy was living with Calvin, one of her mother's old beaus. From what I had heard, he molested her and stole her heart. I guess she felt like anything was better than the hellhole she was living in with Edna. Since Edna was rarely in her right mind, Billie spoke on her behalf. Every time she saw him, she told him that she was going to call the police on his perverted behind. He'd always respond by saying, "Billie, now I done told you, all ya'll got it all wrong. I'm just helping Joy out 'til her mama get right. She don't want to go to no foster home like her brothers. But if you want, I'll kick her out." Billie would tell him that is exactly what she wanted, but then a couple weeks later, we'd hear another rumor about Calvin and Joy. It became evident that he was a liar when Joy came back around pregnant. Word around the projects was that Calvin kicked Joy out when she told him she was with child. He said it wasn't his. Joy had nowhere else to turn so she ended up on her drug-addicted mother's doorstep asking for help. Billie was compelled to ask Joy to stay with her until her mother got herself together, even though Billie feared that day would never come. I think for the first time, I was actually proud of my mother, to know she was thinking of someone other than herself. She spent less time drinking because she was always looking out for Joy. Billie made sure she went to her night classes so she could stay in school while she was pregnant and Billie accompanied her to the Department of Welfare to ensure she'd get money for the baby. My mother was a better parent to Joy than she had ever been to any of us. Maybe it was easier for her because she knew it was not her obligation to do so.

Then came the day when one of Edna's neighbors called an ambulance after seeing her lying naked and bruised on the stairwell. When Edna came out of her stupor, she had to be told that she had been raped because she didn't remember anything that had occurred two days prior to her waking up in the hospital. They enrolled her into a clinic that provided free rehabilitation services for those proven to be in financial despair. Edna was eligible and was immediately accepted into the program. She had already begun withdrawal before even entering. Edna never talked about what she had gone through. All anyone ever knew was Edna came out four months later drug free, just in time for her grandson's birth.

After that, Edna's life changed and her friendship with Billie changed as well. Edna avoided alcohol after she came home. Billie said Edna must've been telling the truth all those years because her stash still seemed to be watered down. She said she might as well stop drinking because it obviously was losing its taste, but she didn't. Without alcohol, Billie no longer saw herself as having anything in common with Edna. In her heart, I believe she was happy Edna was off of drugs and liquor, but she was scared to relinquish her hold on the latter of the two. Billie knew that if she did, she'd have to face the reality of her life… that she was a twenty-five year old drunk with no job, no man and six daughters.

Edna got a job and went to her meetings regularly. Joy moved in with her and Chance and Thurman were given back into her custody. Billie and Edna, although their relationship had diminished drastically, still talked to one another every now and then. The conversations, however, would always end abruptly when Edna urged Billie to come visit her church, give up liquor or be a good mother to us girls. Billie would tell Edna to go to hell and accuse her of being "high and mighty." Then she'd go through the apartment for a few minutes cursing and mumbling.

"Ol' fool finally get her pitiful butt off drugs and now she wanna save the world, her pitiful black butt."

Billie would then vow to never utter another word to Edna. That is, until she was short on food stamps. Then, she'd be banging down Edna's door asking her to spot her a few dollars until the following month. Edna would always come through and though unspoken, it would be understood that "next month" would never come.

My grandparents continued going to church and their faith in the Lord seemed to grow more each week. Rosa would always fall asleep. Her eyes would be bright and wide until we entered the big wooden doors of the church. Then, they'd begin to droop and before my grandmother could give her routine warnings about not dozing on God, she'd be fast asleep; snoring and everything. I spent practically all of my time in church not joining in the songs or listening to the preacher, but praying. I tried to make sense of everything; tried to understand why I had to be born into such a pathetic situation. I'd ask God questions and then I'd pray for my sisters, ask God some more questions and pray for my sisters some more. I remember asking, "Are you there God or did you go on an extended vacation?" Maybe he was just too busy to answer my call, I thought. I better try again later. You see, I felt like Billie might be beyond hope, but I didn't want my sisters to grow up anything like her. Although we had different fathers, I loved them all the same, with the exception of Jackie. I saw my sisters being influenced by our mother's lifestyle and I was extremely angry. They even began talking like her behind closed doors. Rosa and I were eleven and we could already see our seven-year-old sister growing up way too fast. So I prayed and prayed and prayed. All of my grandparents' friends commended me on how attentive I was during service. They said that I was destined to be a preacher. Ha, if they only knew, I hadn't heard a word the preacher had uttered. I didn't even know if I believed in this whole Lord thing, at the time. There was a lot I didn't fully understand, but I heard all the old folks say, "ask and it shall be given." They said there was nothing God could not do, so I put their words to the test and hoped they knew what they were talking about.

Nope, they didn't, I thought as Billie kept right on drinking. My sisters weren't getting any better either. Things just seemed to be getting worse… I should've known better. Shoot, people running around talking to somebody that don't even exist, singing songs to nobody and then thinking their problems would disappear and health would be restored. What a joke, I thought. If there were such a thing as God, surely he wouldn't let little girls suffer the way my sisters had. Sure, Rosa and I were well taken care of, but what about Jackie, Brandy, Gina and Dorothy? I knew I was loved, my grandparents provided for me. But what about a mother who'd bake cookies like the ones on t.v. did; what about the hugs and kisses and long talks? We had a big hole in our hearts. We hadn't asked to be brought into a family where our father would leave us and our mother would be a drunken disgrace. I hated to see my sisters calling every man who entered the door and stayed more than a week, "daddy"; my six and seven-year-old sisters cursing like sailors. All of them were out of control; missing days of school because they had stayed up until 2 a.m. the night before. My grandma used to say, "Who wouldn't serve a God like this," when she heard some good news. My question was, who would?

CHAPTER THREE

DANGEROUS LIASIONS

B illie was really excited about the new guy Edna had introduced her to. She said she had been seeing him for two weeks and he hadn't even tried to kiss her. She didn't know whether to be worried or relieved.

"I hope he ain't no faggot Edna. If he is I swear I'll never speak to you again," she said.

"You just ain't used to having no guy respect you Billie. You been treated like trash so long that you think that's the way it's supposed to be," replied Edna.

I agreed with Edna, but I know Billie would've never listened to me. I really liked Eddie. He was the first man since my father left that I truly liked. He was funny just like daddy. Eddie was a good friend of Edna's fiancé, Joseph. She had met both men in one of her support group meetings and they were also members at Grace Fellowship Tabernacle, Edna's church. Edna and Joseph had hit it off immediately. So much so, that he proposed just three months after their first date.

I have to admit I was actually happy when Eddie came to the door with his brown suitcase and his two garbage bags, wearing that sheepish grin. He even slept on the couch for the first month "out of respect for the kids." After many attitudes and attempts at seduction, he finally gave in and moved into the bedroom permanently.

Eddie took us to the park and museums. He said it wasn't good to keep kids in the ghetto all of the time. You have to let them see that there's more to the world than the projects, he would tell Billie. That's something that I've never forgotten. Eddie's words taught me a great deal. You have to broaden your horizons. You can't confine people to certain limits and expect them to perform beyond them.

I should've known it wouldn't last, I was too happy. I had finally found some peace. No more drunken stupors to deal with; no snotty nose girls to baby-sit. For the first time, I began to think maybe there was a God and he had finally answered my prayer. For the first time, I understood what grandma Helen meant when she used to say, "The Lord may not come when you want him, but he's always right on time." My sisters liked Eddie too. When he came home from work, they'd all come out running and yelling, "Ed, Ed." Billie's rent was paid on time and she always had food on the table. For a year, Billie's household seemed normal. Eddie even talked of marrying Billie. They had spent an entire day looking at rings once. Then that day came that I shall never forget. It was a Friday evening and Rosa and I had just arrived for our weekend visitation. Eddie walked through the door. I could tell immediately that he wasn't his usual self. He looked in our direction, but it was as if he didn't even see us. Without even taking off his coat, he plopped down on the couch. My sisters ran to him as was their routine, but instead of grabbing them and smothering their faces with kisses, he snapped, "Come on now, get off me. I had a hard day." We later discovered the reason behind his hostility. Eddie had lost his job. Some things were discovered missing at the warehouse where he worked. Eddie's boss knew about his past drug addiction and that, along with the color of his skin, made him a prime suspect for the crime. Without a trial, he had been accused, prosecuted and found guilty. Eddie died on that day. For a few weeks after that he tried to handle the situation. Joseph had given him a pep talk and as a result, he had made up his mind to have faith that something else would come along.

Eddie had been a faithful churchgoer when he met Billie. He had even urged her to come visit Grace Tabernacle, but she always refused. "You need to find Jesus before it's too late," he'd tell her. "Why, is he lost," she'd sarcastically respond. They say friends can either draw you or drive you to God. In Eddie's case, the latter was true. As they grew closer, he drifted further from the church. Even though I had my doubts about church and God, I was mature enough to realize that faith did have a positive effect on some people. It had changed Edna's life completely and my grandparents were the kindest people I ever knew. I was upset when Billie sucked the faith from Eddie. To this day, I believe that if he had remained an active member, he would've been equipped to fight off the self-pity that was slowly overtaking him. What was it about Billie that drained a man and left him defenseless against life's obstacles?

Everyday he went out looking for work, but he was either overqualified or underqualified. It didn't help either that he had a criminal record. He had once been arrested after he tried to steal an elderly woman's pocketbook in an attempt to get quick cash for drugs. Every weekend we'd come over and it seemed like a little more of his soul had diminished...until finally there was nothing left. He'd just lay around on the couch in dingy gray sweat pants. A beard began to invade his face and even on the days when he did wash, he still looked dirty. We all had to walk on eggshells in his presence for fear that we'd be the next targets of his rage. He never hit anyone, he'd just yell until the walls shook. Then he started to be missing for days at a time. Billie had to know what was going on, but she refused to believe it. He'd come back from his excursion energetic and unbelievably joyful. We didn't ask questions, we were just happy to have the old Ed back, regardless of how he got there. Then things began to be missing. The clock, the silver cups Billie and my daddy had gotten as a wedding gift from Grandma Helen and Grandpa George. There were times when money would be missing. Billie would ask my sisters and I to give up the culprit and when we swore that none of us had taken it, she'd beat us for lying.

One morning Billie had taken Rosa, Jackie and I with her to the store. She had left the others with Edna. I remember feeling really close to Billie that day. We all stopped for ice cream and talked and laughed. We took the bus home and Billie sent Jackie down the hall to get the others. She put the key in the lock and opened the door. Our mouths hung open in shock. I could not believe it. Where was her couch, her kitchen table, her chairs?? Billie frantically ran from room to room. She had been cleaned out. Even that old pine dresser and prickly blue rug had been stolen out of Billie's bedroom. The toys in my sisters' bedroom were all that had been left. Good ol' Ed, a humanitarian to the end!

I ran to get Edna. She came over and could do nothing but shake her head. "Lord, this is a terrible thing, a terrible thing," she cried, "He must've come in here with a moving crew from the looks of things." That's exactly what he had done. He owed some dangerous men a lot of money, so as a down payment, he gave them permission to take "his" things and sell them.

We never saw Eddie again.

I wish I could say that was the worst things ever got, but it wasn't. I don't know why Billie didn't just give up on love; it would've made life easier for everyone. Instead, she continued to get involved in one bad relationship after another…sometimes simultaneously. Her liaisons were getting scary. I remember a woman coming to the door threatening Billie with a knife. She promised to kill her if she didn't stop seeing her husband. My mother, obviously intoxicated, laughed in her face. She told the lady to tell the man to leave her alone. "You can have him back anyway, I think he's broken in enough now," she taunted. Billie still bears a scar on the left side of her face where the woman slashed her. I remember Brandy, Jackie and I jumping between her and Billie as Gina and Dorothy begged the scorned woman not to kill our mother. Rosa just sat on the floor with her thumb in her mouth. Without saying a word, she seemed to be cheering the woman on.

My twin sister loathed our mother. The only people she hated more were our sisters. She never called them by name, she'd simply say, "those bad kids," when referring to them and she labeled Billie, "that woman." Rosa never played with our siblings when we visited. She'd bring books to read, paper to write. She even hated the fact that they shared our last name. The surrounding was completely inadequate as far as Rosa was concerned. She would even hold her urine until she was about to bust because she did not want to use Billie's bathroom. When she'd have to give in to her bladder, she'd cover the toilet bowl with tissue like grandma had taught us to do when using public restrooms. She was more than satisfied with our middle-class upbringing and never understood why we had to visit Billie anyway.

I had noticed Rosa's extreme behavior before, but I didn't know the extent of her dislike toward our mother until one day I told my sister she should try to love Billie. After all, she was our mother. Rosa had a fit…literally. She was screaming and shaking uncontrollably. "Don't you ever say that. She is not my mother. Don't say that, don't say that!" I was so shocked by her reaction that I didn't know how to respond at first, but I finally promised to never bring the subject up again.

Grandma Helen must've picked up on Rosa's feelings because she sat us both down and had a long talk with us. Grandma told us that we didn't have to visit Billie if we didn't want to. "You don't have to feel obligated just because she's your mother. You'll never have to do something you don't feel comfortable with." Before she could finish her sentence, Rosa had confided that she never wanted to go back. I'd have to make the weekend visits alone.

I wasn't angry with my sister. There were times when I wished I had the guts to leave and never look back. Like the night my mother got into an argument with a guest at one of the rowdy parties she was hosting. I'm not sure how the dispute began. I just remember running out of my sisters' room after hearing yelling and glass shattering. There some man stood brandishing a broken liquor bottle at Billie. He was so drunk, he could barely stand. He finally stumbled, landing on his butt. Some of Billie's "friends" took the weapon out of his hand and dragged him out of the door by his feet. Needless to say, I never complained about being bored on the weekend.

Billie eventually lost interest in married men and those already committed in relationships. She then turned her attention to more "passionate" men. That is, men whose passion was to put their hands on her. I guess she had sunk to an all time low. She felt like garbage so she allowed them to treat her as such. When we'd come to visit, I wouldn't know what to expect. Would she have a black eye or a bruised arm, a swollen lip? Billie would always stop seeing the men after they began beating her, but I still feared for her safety. One day I realized my fears were justified.

Billie's new beau, Robby, spent many nights at her apartment. All five of us were frightened by his presence. He was a tall, dark-skinned man with a baldhead and he always bore a frown. He also had a slight limp and walked with a cane. It was made of the darkest, heaviest wood I'd ever seen and it was carved in such a way that it looked like a snake was wrapped around it. The handle was in the image of a snake's head. It must've weighed about five pounds. He gave me such a creepy feeling that I wouldn't visit if I knew he was going to be there.

I was devastated when Grandma Helen told me Billie was in the hospital, clinging on to life. Besides the external bumps and bruises, she had sustained internal injuries. Grandma said I could no longer visit my mother. She said she refused to keep putting me in harm's way. God had lent us to her, she cried, and she would protect us to the best of her ability. So my visits with my mother ceased and it would be years before I'd see her again or find out how she had landed in the hospital on the brink of death.

I would eventually be told about Robby and Billie's planned evening alone. Edna allowed her to bring my sisters over her house for the night. Billie and her "friend" enjoyed a night filled with sex, lies and Johnny Walker Red. Since he had purchased the alcohol, they both agreed he should get to indulge in the last ounce, but he had fallen asleep. He awoke to find Billie passed out on the bed and the liquor gone. I guess he must've felt betrayed because he beat Billie until she was bloody and when his hands grew weary, he picked up that cane and beat her until she became a shell of the woman she once was. No one knows how she survived the night lying on the floor in a pool of her own blood. Edna had not found her until the next day. The apartment door was cracked when she had come to see if it was all right to let the girls return home.

"Thank God I came when I did," Edna said holding her heart, "God truly watches over babes and fools."

After recovering from a pierced lung and a fractured skull, Billie moved with Edna's help. She didn't want to take a chance that Robby might return to finish the job. When Rosa learned of Billie's complete recovery, she only said three words, "That's too bad."

CHAPTER 4

HELL CHANGES THINGS

No one can prepare you for the death of a loved one, especially when you're just a child and that loved one is your only source of strength and guidance. There's nothing anyone can say or do that will ease the pain that accompanies the words, "They're gone. I'm sorry the doctors did all they could."

When Grandma Helen and Grandpa George died, I really thought I would lose my mind. After all, they had raised Rosa and I. No one could ever take the place of my God-loving, self-esteem building, self-sacrificing grandparents.

They had left my sister and I in the house while they went to pick up some necessary items at the grocery store. All the television channels were broadcasting special reports about the imminent blizzard. The snowfall was already heavy and the streets slippery, but the anchors informed the viewers that the storm was just beginning. I began to worry when my grandparents hadn't returned after a couple hours. The store was only a few miles from our home. My stomach began to feel jittery and my heart seemed to beat a little faster. I knew something had happened. To this day, I can't explain how I knew. I remember that I felt the way I had when it began to get dark outside and daddy had not come back from the store. Billie had insisted we sit in the window and wait, but I knew he wasn't coming back...just as I knew I wasn't going to ever see my grandparents again.

When Aunt Lizzy came to the house later that night, her expression said it all. She tried to smile, but she couldn't. She told us how she had gotten a call from the pastor of their church. The hospital had called him because both of my grandparents had church cards in their wallets and grandpa had always carried one of those miniature duplicates of his deacon's license. Pastor Banks did not want to call the house. Upon finding out Rosa and I weren't in the car, he didn't want to risk calling the house and being forced to tell us about the tragedy over the phone. Instead, he notified my aunt.

I felt like dying too. I can't tell you how many times I had wished I had been in the car. How sad, a fifteen-year-old girl miserable because she is alive. I wanted to die, but I had to survive...for Rosa. I had to survive to help her because the next three years, which we spent living in Billie's home, can only be comparable to hell.

My aunt Lizzy had six kids of her own and her husband, Uncle Rich, just wasn't keen on the idea of taking in two more. Especially when the two had a mother, who in his words, "had been getting off scott free for years." My father only had the one sibling so Billie was our only choice. Not to mention the fact that, during the two weeks we had stayed with my aunt, Billie had petitioned the courts to get us back into her custody. It had been three years since either one of us had seen her. Maybe she thought she could get her hands on the money my grandparents had left us in their will. She knew they had left us something, but she wasn't sure exactly how much. Anyway, she couldn't get it. We couldn't even touch the trust funds until we turned 21.

I still remember the day my aunt told us that Mr. Silverstein, my grandparent's attorney, wanted to see us. Rosa and I got all dressed up and my aunt took us to his office. There, he told us that my grandparents had been concerned about our futures. In their will, they named Aunt Lizzy and my dad as their sole beneficiaries. Trustees had been assigned to find my dad after my grandparents died but they returned empty- handed. Grandma Helen and Grandpa George left my aunt and her husband their house, but they had opened trust funds for us. The instructions they left stated that we could not get the money until we reached a certain age unless we needed it for college, then we could collect the money after our eighteenth birthday. Together, the funds were $150,000-75 thousand dollars a piece.

Our lives had changed. Needless to say, Billie could not afford the parochial school we attended so we had to transfer to public school. Rosa and I were accustomed to having our own rooms. Now we had to learn to share a room with Dorothy. Gina, Brandy and Jackie shared the other bedroom. After Billie was attacked, she moved into a three-bedroom apartment on Clinton Avenue, a street plagued with drugs and crime. Liquor stores, bars and check cashing places adorned almost every corner. Abandoned buildings, rubble and bus stops seemed to make up the remaining area. This section of Newark had once thrived, but the riots had changed that. There had been clothing stores and supermarkets on the street before some white police officers dragged a black man out of a cab and beat him. The incident followed Martin Luther King's assassination and black folks were already pissed off with the country. Tension and frustration peaked and residents began looting and burning buildings and businesses down in their own communities. My grandparents had raised us in what was referred to as the Weequahic section of Newark. We had lived in a four bedroom brick colonial home surrounded by wealthy white folks. My grandfather had worked at the General Motors plant in Linden for nearly twenty years before retiring and my grandmother had been a high school teacher. Needless to say, Rosa and I experienced culture shock when we were forced to move into Billie's tiny apartment. Billie was extremely proud of her new place. You would've thought she had moved to Beverly Hills the way she talked about it.

Rosa blamed herself for our grandparents' death, even though I always reminded her that she wasn't driving the truck that had run the stop sign and slammed into them. She had been painting her fingernails when the phone rang the day my grandparents were killed. I was in the bathroom and yelled for her to answer it, but she said she couldn't risk messing up her fingernail polish. By the time I got it, it had stopped ringing. After we found out that Grandma Helen and Grandpa George were dead, Rosa said they had probably been rushing home to see if we were O.K. She said it had probably been them who called when she didn't answer the phone because they had a habit of calling and checking up on us if they had left us alone for a while in the house.

"If they hadn't been driving fast, they probably would've seen the truck in time," she'd always say.

Even though Rosa's theory was nothing but speculation, she had convinced herself it was an accurate account of that day's tragic events. To punish herself and to protest the deck fate had unjustly dealt us, she stopped speaking. Rosa wouldn't talk to anyone, but me. Everyone in our new school thought she was deaf and mute.

There was one television in Billie's apartment, but it was in the living room so we could never watch it because Billie was always "entertaining." It wouldn't have mattered to Rosa anyway because she would come home, stay in that room we shared and study. Most of the time, she wouldn't even eat. She began to lose weight and it seemed to me that she rarely ever slept, but she kept getting excellent grades.

I had watched Rosa study herself into insomnia, but I didn't know it was all part of a plan until the day she came into the apartment, went straight up to Billie, opened her mouth and said, "I'm leaving. Today. Right now." Rosa had told me a couple weeks prior that she had gotten a full scholarship to Stanford University. We both had applied to numerous colleges, even though Billie had assured us it was a waste of time. She said we should look for work so we could help her out. After all, she had taken us in during our time of need. Rosa and I applied to all of the same colleges, except Stanford. I had not even considered getting an application. I had been so busy working 50 hours a week at the mall and trying to keep peace at Billie's that I had let my grades slip. I was overwhelmed just to learn that I had gotten accepted to Rutgers on partial scholarship. When Rosa told me about her acceptance letter from Stanford, I saw a twinkle in her eye and for the first time in nearly three years, I saw her smile. For the first time ever, we were going to be going our separate ways. I was crushed, but I had managed to smile back. What I didn't know was my sister had saved up enough money to buy a one-way plane ticket and now just when graduation was right around the corner, she was ready to forfeit her rightful place as valedictorian to hop on a plane to

California. She had signed up for summer orientation so she could live in the dorms until school began.

"I'm exempt from finals. Why should I stay Angie?" she asked

"For me, maybe"

"I cannot stay in this hell hole one more minute. I love you Angie, but if I stay here I might as well put the razor to my wrists now because that's what I'll end up doing…killing myself. So, I either stay here and you bury me too or I leave and live!"

My sister had been silent for three years, but at that moment I can recall that all I wanted her to do was shut-up.

So she left. She called a taxi and rode out of my life. She didn't say goodbye to Billie or any of the girls. She just hugged me like it was the last time and without looking back, she got inside the yellow cab and rode away. If I was going to survive now, it would have to be for myself.

CHAPTER 5

RELATED DOESN'T MEAN RELATIONSHIP

B randy was always cordial to Billie, but they didn't really have a relationship. In the back of my mind, I always felt like she simply tolerated our mother…or maybe, she was simply apathetic. Jackie and Billie had bonded early. They seemed more like friends than mother and daughter. I don't think Jackie saw Billie as an authoritative figure in her life deserving of respect, but instead, as a girlfriend with whom she could exchange gossip. I had witnessed moments in Billie's household when she and Jackie argued. I had shuddered in disbelief and fear as Jackie, then thirteen, yelled, "kiss my butt" to our mother. I remember standing back. I didn't want to be in the way when she got smacked in the mouth or worse. However, all that followed was Billie's rebuttal, "No, you kiss mine."

Billie had always swept up behind Gina's messes and it seemed that was the extent of their relationship. When Gina got pregnant, Billie acted as if she had expected it. "Don't worry, we'll get you on welfare," was her nonchalant response. No speech about how disappointed she was or words of wisdom regarding what was to come.

Billie always expressed love for Dorothy. The rare occasions when she was home, she would hug her and kiss her and even sit down next to her and play in her hair. However, by the time Dorothy was born, our mother had completely thrown herself into partying. Even though it was obvious that she was fond of "her baby", Dorothy was loved from a distance most of the time. After entering puberty, Brandy, Gina and Jackie would often accompany Billie on her escapades while Dorothy was left at home. Ironically, Billie seemed to want more for her. I tried to be there for my youngest sister, but by the time she reached adolescence, I was trying to make a life for myself. We did, however, grow close and I managed to be around when she needed me most. I think she's always known she could count on Billie's love...and my presence.

While Billie looked the other way when my sisters erred, she went out of her way to point out my mistakes. When I chose to go to college in spite of her advice, she made me feel guilty. I can still hear her saying, "Go ahead, go ahead, abandon the family just like your father did. You're just like him!" I'd never do that and I was determined to prove my mother wrong. When I graduated from college and got a job, Billie didn't congratulate me. Instead she said, "Insurance? That's kinda boring ain't it?" As if I was going to be traveling door to door wearing white shoes and a matching belt. She, like most people, didn't know there was another side to the insurance industry-commercial insurance. Businesses and corporations took out policies for everything under the sun. I'd have to underwrite those policies, deal with insurance brokers and grow my renewal book of business with new written premium. Billie hadn't asked me what I'd be doing. It didn't matter anyway. There was no accomplishment grand enough to render her pride.

I used to wonder how Billie would have responded if I had chosen a more glamorous profession. What if I had pursued an acting career and ended up winning an Oscar? Would she have loved me then? Probably not. I'm sure she would have willingly lived off of my fame but I doubt that it would have influenced her level of affection. For, I had earned countless awards in college and countless more in my industry and none of them had stirred a desirable response out of my mother. Twice I had even invited her to awards dinners. Each time, I had hoped, with every ounce of my being, that she would accept my invitation and every time, she hadn't bothered to show up. In fact, she hadn't even thought my invitation worthy of any response at all. I'd ask her to come and she'd just look at me as if I had spoken in a foreign language, before returning to whatever she had been previously doing.

I didn't talk about Billie to Rosa but once during a phone conversation, I mentioned Billie's lack of enthusiasm regarding my achievements. Rosa ignored me at first. We had agreed never to discuss her. Then she said abruptly, "She's just jealous of you. You are everything she always wished she could be, but never was." How could a mother be jealous of her own daughter, I wondered. Instead of choosing to be envious, wouldn't she choose to live vicariously through her offspring? Rosa didn't explain further, she changed the subject-reminding me we had breached our agreement, without saying a word. Even though I thought her statement had no merit, it remained in my subconscious. I have always believed that Billie's disregard for my feelings has been due to either ignorance or the fact that she's blamed me for my father's departure. Rosa's not around so she can't take it out on her. I don't know if I'll ever discover the true reason behind her resentment.

Before graduating from Rutgers, I managed to get up the nerve to question Billie about her blatant decision to relate to each of us differently. I told her I needed a relationship with her even if my siblings didn't. I'll never forget her eloquent reply, "I love my kids, all my kids, but just `cause we're related don't mean we got to have a relationship."

CHAPTER 6

JACKIE

"**M**y friend Selena called me today crying about the things her boyfriend is putting her through. I don't know why she's so surprised when he acts up. Shoot, he works at the car wash. I told her like I tell everybody, a man is only worth how much he makes."

Jackie's comment did not go unheard. It was accompanied by Billie's feverish laughter. Jackie ran over to our mother and they slapped hands in approval. Jackie, who stood tall at five feet nine inches, was wearing a red spandex halter-top and a pair of tight black Calvin Klein jeans. Her thick long hair rested on her back and her manicured hands, on her hips. The diamond stud earrings in her ear glistened as she spoke. I didn't have to ask if they were the real thing. Just knowing Jackie, I knew they were. She was the only unemployed 25-year-old I knew driving a brand new convertible BMW.

I just stood there watching her and Billie bond. I think Jackie had a certain boldness that Billie admired. After all, she had slept with numerous men in her lifetime and all she got for it was one heartache after another. At least Jackie was getting "paid" for her services. Yep, Billie never said it, but I know she had thought it more than once.

"Billie, what kind of message are you sending to Jackie," I said, interrupting, "Jackie, you need to learn how to take care of yourself and stop depending on some man to do it for you."

"Here we go again," she said, "I am so sick and tired of your lectures...always trying to tell somebody how to run their life. Where's your man? Hey, maybe that's it. Maybe you just jealous."

Jealous of what? I thought. Sure, she drove a nice car, had tons of jewelry and designer clothes and she took luxury vacations twice a year. If she pawned it all, she still wouldn't have enough to purchase my dignity and self-respect.

"Look, I am not going to argue with you Jackie. Do what you want. All I'm saying is that if you keep up this pace, it won't be long before you'll be on the street with the rest of the hoes."

I immediately left the room, bearing a huge grin. I knew I had just uttered "fighting words" so I grabbed my jacket and walked to the door. "Bye Billie," I said closing the door behind me. I could hear Jackie cursing in the background. We had always shared an extremely antagonistic relationship. After my grandparents' died and I moved in with Billie, I kind of took over as mother. Of course, as my sisters grew up they still did whatever they wanted, but they always sought my advice. When they were young, they all gave me respect. Everyone, except Jackie. Even now, although my sisters are all grown up, they respect me. Everyone, except Jackie. I guess we've always had a mutual disgust for one another.

CHAPTER 7

GINA

F our kids!! Now, she was coming to my house crying saying she was pregnant again. We could barely make out Gina's words as she sat at the kitchen table, her head resting in her hands and snot oozing out of her fingers like shampoo.

"You're what?" Billie asked, "Somebody give her a tissue so we can hear what the heck she's talking about."

Gina's story was one all of us had heard four times prior. She was always in love and was always "about" to get married. That is until she'd turn up pregnant. The men? She'd always meet the ones that were just getting on their feet. You know the type. They'd move into her two-bedroom apartment while they looked for something they could afford. It's amazing how quickly they'd find something as soon as she shared the joyous news with them. Gina was worse than the nice old lady down the street who always welcomed strays into her home. They'd somehow end up on the side of her home. She'd feed the cats and they'd keep coming back until finally they refused to ever leave. Gina had fallen into the same trap over and over again. Thank God, she didn't have babies by every man who had at one time or another rested his shoes under her bed. If she had, she'd be on her way to claiming a spot in the Guineas Book of World Records. Four men had not been so lucky. They had left her with something to remember them. My twenty-three year old sister had three sons and a daughter, all under the age of eight. Once again, she had come to tell us her family was expanding. Ironically, Billie ended up with all of the kids. She said she couldn't stand to see her grandchildren cramped up in some tiny, roach-infested apartment so she kept them in *my* house.

Seven years ago, I secured a job with an insurance company right out of college. Promotions followed and the pay was quite competitive. I had moved out of Billie's shortly after Rosa left, but it wasn't until five years ago that I took some of the money my grandparents left me and bought a house. I had only used a small amount of the money for college. The house, which was located in the beautiful suburb of Maplewood, was a beautiful black and white four bedroom, two and a half bath colonial with a huge attic and finished basement, similar to the one I grew up in. Billie had stopped drinking a couple years prior and she was really struggling since she didn't have any dependent children and no check coming in every month. I moved Billie, Gina and her kids (she only had two then) in with me. I fixed the basement up really nice. I bought a bedroom set, a color television and a sofa and love seat so Billie could have a bedroom and a sitting area down there. Brandy was already on her own, Dorothy was living with her boyfriend and Jackie was some business tycoon's mistress. He had her set up in her own condo so she could be accessible to him at all times. Gina left my house but Billie had invited her kids to stay after she got pregnant for the third time. Now, all four of her kids lived with us, and she was telling me we should expect another?

I wanted to scream but I didn't utter a sound. I should've anticipated it I guess but I wanted to believe Gina had learned her lesson. A month ago she was practically glowing during one of her visits with her kids. She said she had been seeing some guy she met on the bus.

"I think this might be the one Angela," she had told me, "He's got a job and everything and he loves kids. He's got two of his own."

Did Gina really think she and this guy were going to be the next Brady Bunch? I thought. I tried to listen and be supportive. She said he was an independent contractor. Unemployed, I said to myself. Gina told me he traveled a lot, but he wanted to make New Jersey his permanent home. He's homeless, I thought, and he wants to stay with her rent-free. This Tony guy fit into the same category as all of the men to whom Gina gave her heart and body. He was like a stick of gum placed in a huge box and then wrapped in beautiful paper and topped with a pretty bow…wonderful to look upon but nothing substantial. Now, she was having his baby.

"You should just get rid of it," Jackie interjected, "You gotta stop sometime. If you don't, you're going to have a daycare. You're never going to get a man to take care of you with all these rug rats running around."

"Leave it to you to be sensitive and caring," I yelled.

"That's the problem. Everybody's been too sensitive and caring. Gina doesn't need a hug, she needs a kick in the butt and some birth control pills."

I couldn't even open my mouth to argue. I couldn't bring myself to think of some clever, sarcastic comment. For the first time, maybe ever, Jackie was absolutely right. I know I have always been there for Gina; always gentle and compassionate. Perhaps, because I understood what plagued her and somehow I felt responsible.

I still remember that night. Billie was off on one of her drunken escapades with some of her drunk friends. Brandy and Jackie, just barely teenagers, were out with her. Rosa and Dorothy slept in our room and Gina was in the other room alone. When I heard the knock at the door, I started to just ignore it. I had already turned about five people away-telling them Billie wasn't home. But, against my better judgment, I asked who it was, with my ear peeled to the door waiting for a response. It was Tucker-Billie's latest beau. He had been to the apartment several times, when Billie was home and when she wasn't, so there was nothing unusual about him asking if he could come in and wait for Billie. Now, I remember Grandma Helen always warned, "never open the door for strangers" but Tucker was no stranger, so I let him in. I sat down in the living room with him for a little while and watched television. Then, I went back to my room to finish some homework. I must've dozed off. I woke up in a daze and immediately decided to see if Billie had come home or if Tucker was still waiting. I walked down the short hall and I remember hearing strange noises coming from Gina's room a few feet away. The door wasn't completely shut. I peeked in and I saw

Tucker's body moving. Shadows danced on the wall. I opened the door and the tears fell before my mouth did. Thirteen-year-old Gina lay flat on the bed, her face in the pillow. She dare not cry aloud. I ran to the kitchen and retrieved a butcher knife. Tucker had been so preoccupied; he hadn't seen me in the doorway. All I remember is running toward him. A loud moan seemed to rise up from my soul. He must've run because I raised my hand a few times, heard him scream and then the front door slam. I must've stabbed him pretty good because a small pool of blood covered the floor.

I never asked any questions. I just picked up my half-naked sister and rocked her in my arms as if she were a babe. I stroked her hair and whispered the only thing that came to my mind, "It's over." I don't know how long Tucker had been raping my sister nor do I know why he chose her out of my mother's six daughters. I do know that even though he never beat her during the molestation, he wounded her so deeply that she has never recovered.

Gina begged me not to tell Billie what I had witnessed. She said she'd get in trouble because our mother would blame her for doing something to entice Tucker. Sadly, Gina was probably right so I cleaned up the blood and never mentioned that night again.

I later learned that Tucker hadn't been the first of Billie's boyfriends, who after being invited into her apartment, helped himself to Gina.

CHAPTER 8

BRANDY

She always seemed to have everything together. She had never gotten excellent grades but she did well enough to graduate high school and land a job with a post office in an affluent town, making good money…great money, without a college degree. Shortly after getting that job, she moved out of Billie's and she's been living alone ever since. Yep, Brandy had seemed to escape the awful curse Billie had passed down to all of her kids. She wasn't scandalous. As a matter of fact, Brandy was almost as bad as me when it came to having a man. Sure, I'd hear about a date she had here or there but she never got serious with anyone. Maybe she hadn't escaped after all. My sister had such confidence that it was easy to believe that she had planned her life that way; that her life was actually better for not having a steady beau. She was independent.

That's why I was so worried about her when she lost her job. She remained extremely tight-lipped about why she showed up for work one day and was told never to return. She finally said she had been laid off. I knew since she wouldn't be working for a while, it wouldn't be long before Brandy found herself struggling to pay rent, her car note, credit card bills and buy groceries. I was so worried about her that I began to lose sleep. I know how hard it is for someone to be accustomed to a certain way of life and then have everything altered suddenly so I asked her to come live with me, Billie and the kids. At first she turned me down but several months passed and she could not find a job so she reluctantly moved in. She agreed to stay here until she finds another job and gets on her feet.

Brandy is so unpredictable. Maybe I never noticed it before or maybe she had just recently become that way. I can't remember a time when Brandy had so many mood swings. She'd be in the kitchen talking to the rest of the family one minute and then the next minute, she'd be sitting alone silently in a corner of the family room. Must be the whole job thing, I thought, that can definitely make a person act a little strange.

Besides the moodiness, I was getting along just fine with Brandy. She washed dishes and cooked. Shoot, it was nice coming home to a cooked meal. I see what men mean. When it had just been Billie in the house I always had to call home before I left work to see what kind of fast food everyone wanted. Billie only cooked on special occasions and needless to say, with four children in the house, Ronald McDonald became our personal chef.

Eventually, Brandy seemed to just stop looking for work. She seemed content just collecting her unemployment checks. I don't know what she did on the weekdays, but on the weekend, she'd sleep until 2 p.m.. Then, she'd leave and we wouldn't see her again until late that night; actually, we didn't see her then. She'd always come in after everyone was asleep. I'd always know she was home when I'd hear the door to her room shut. This weekend had followed the same script.

Speaking of weekends, they go by way too quickly. It seems like I go to sleep Friday night and wake up to Monday. Mondays are always horrible for me. I can never get my bearings until Tuesday. Today was exceptionally bad. I had an argument with one of the brokers with whom I do business and I spilled coffee on my one and only Donna Karan blouse. No, not just a drip; I mean I practically spilled the entire cup down my shirt. It was much hotter than I had anticipated and when I stuck my lip in it, my hand trembled-that was all she wrote. To make matters worse, we had a branch meeting this morning…shortly after the coffee fiasco. It's difficult to think of clever things to say when you look like Dirty Linus from the Peanuts gang.

To my surprise and misfortune, that was not the horrifying peak to my day. I put on my jacket and decided to reward myself for sticking out the day by going to my favorite deli around the corner from my job. My mouth watered as I imagined myself eating a pastrami on rye. Shoot, I deserved it. I could've taken half a day-I should've taken half a day. On my way to the deli, I bumped into Yolanda Watkins. Oooh, I can't stand her. She grew up in the projects but you'd think she was the princess of Bel Air the way she walks around with her nose in the air. Maybe I can act like I don't see her, I thought...uh-oh, too late. She was flagging me down like an air traffic controller.

"Hey, Yolanda. How are you?"

"Oh, I'm doing great, I work the night shift tonight so I figured I'd get some shopping done before I go in. Oh, did you know I just got engaged. You know Larry right?"

"Uh-ye"

"Well, he's such a great guy," she interrupted, "I would show you my ring, but after putting it on my finger, he said the diamond wasn't big enough for his baby so he took it back. He's going to exchange it for a bigger one. Isn't that sweet?"

This coming from someone who thought carats were something Bugs Bunny ate. I didn't bother to answer. I knew Yolanda long enough to know that when she asked you a question she didn't expect you to answer. She must've thought her raspy, nasal voice was beautiful because she wouldn't shut up. She must've also thought I was crazy if she thought I believed her for a minute about the whole ring drama. My girlfriend Tammy was friends with Yolanda's cousin and she told her that Yolanda's boyfriend had been arrested for theft. I don't doubt he gave her a ring but he probably wanted her to fence it, not wear it.

"Well, I have to go. I have to head back to the office soon," I finally said.

"Yeah, girl me too," she quickly responded.

Yeah, the post office, I thought, back to licking stamps you go. They must keep her in one of the back rooms with her ghetto self. I can't believe she's a federal employee.

"Oh and tell Brandy I'm sorry about her getting fired and all. That's really too bad."

The words hit me like a brick. Fired? Brandy? No, Yolanda must've been trying to get to me like she always did. She had always been jealous of me so every time I ran into her, she had something negative to say...disguised as something positive. The last time I was unfortunate enough to bump into Ms. Yolanda, she told me, "Ooo girl, you looking good." I should've known better than to smile. She continued, "That extra weight really becomes you. I could never let myself go like that. My man likes things very particular. It must be nice not to have a man to answer to. You can do your hair any way you like, gain as much weight as you want..." That time I said I had to go and walked away before she could finish her put down. Before our last encounter, I had been thinking I looked a little chunkier-my hips appeared to be spreading. Sometimes, I think they have a mind of their own. I had shrugged it off, I figured I must be retaining water because it was almost that time of the month. How nice of Yolanda to notice too. It was just like that witch to point out things you really didn't want to know or was trying hard to deny. Now, she was implying that my sister had been fired. It couldn't be. She was just trying to piss me off as usual. I decided right at that moment that I was not going to play along. I ignored what she had just told me.

"Brandy's doing great. I'll tell her you asked about her. Well, I have to go. Oh and by the way, I hope Larry gets out real soon. Keep hope alive!"

And with that, I strolled away, my head held high and my chest slightly protruding. Hey, this is not such a bad day after all, I thought.

CHAPTER 9

A HOUSE DIVIDED

I stood in the doorway watching my home get smaller and smaller. How did I let this happen? How could I have allowed things to get this much out of hand?

"Excuse us Angie," Jackie said as she slightly nudged me to the side. The movers followed her to the attic carrying the headboard and frame of her brass bed. She had accumulated a lot of things over the years. I would've never had enough room to accommodate her but Brandy had offered to share her rented storage unit with Jackie as long as she was willing to share the bill.

I came home Wednesday and Billie told me Bob had given Jackie the boot. She had been his 'other woman' for years. I never understood why that white man chose to mess around with Jackie. I had always heard that all white men have fantasies about being with a black woman but it wasn't like Jackie had class or anything. Sure, she was beautiful to look at but her assets stopped there. What did they talk about, I had often wondered. They couldn't possibly have anything in common. Maybe they didn't talk. Well, whatever they did, they wouldn't be doing it anymore.

I remember when they first got together. Jackie was working in some club in New York. That was her first and only job. She claimed she was a hostess, but knowing my sister she was probably doing some hoochie coochie dance in a cage or something similar. It seemed like she hadn't even been there a month when she told Billie she was moving out on her own. Before the end of the following month, she had quit her job and was living in one of the most exclusive high rises in New York. I knew immediately what was going on but it was a year and a half later before I discovered he was white.

Jackie would ridicule his wife whenever she and Billie talked, "Where does the stupid heifer think he is when we go on cruises? She's either in denial or just plain dumb."

Jackie did learn a few things from good ol' Bob. Once she had said, "I know better than to ever get in a marriage when the man controls all of the money." She said if Bob had let his wife keep tab on the finances, she would've known that something funny was going on. If she had seen statements, she would've found out that Bob bought Jackie expensive jewelry and a new car every other year, among other things. Jackie was never a proponent of marriage anyway. She'd say, "If I ever get married, I'm not saying all those old vows. I will only say four words…Show Me the Cash!!"

Well, Bob's wife wasn't that stupid. Evidently, she had found out about his secret love affair and had given him quite an ultimatum-either he dump the ho in the condo or she was taking half. Jackie wasn't worth alimony.

After I learned of Jackie's rejection, I didn't feel badly for her and in a moment of unusual cruelty, I said, "Oh well, Bob will have himself another slut this time next month." I wanted to snatch the words back after I heard them leave my mouth. Maybe Jackie really cared about Bob; maybe she was hurt and feeling rejected. That was wrong for me to say, I thought, but before I could apologize, she replied. "Next month? Girl, you must not realize how rich he is. He'll have someone else this time next week. No hard feelings though. I got what I wanted out of the relationship. Now it's time to move on to the next sucker-I mean, man," she chuckled, " Anyway he won't find a better ho than me. Mark my words, Bob will be back and when he comes a calling, I'll do a little more milking."

The girl never ceases to amaze me. Sometimes, I think she's some kind of mutant because she has no feelings. Every time I begin to think I can't loathe her anymore than I already do, she does something to make me more disgusted and who the heck does Billie think she is, inviting her to stay here. She should be thanking God

I've allowed her to stay this long. No, but that's not enough. She's got to keep welcoming all of her dysfunctional daughters-along with their mess- into my home. I should tell her off; I should tell her exactly what I think of her and my sorry siblings. I should let loose on her butt and tell her what a pitiful, perverse, pathetic, poor-excuse for a mother I think she really is!

"Angie, Jackie wants to know where she should put her Mustafa china and crystal," said Billie, interrupting my thoughts.

"I think that's Mikasa. I'm coming Billie."

CHAPTER 10

DOROTHY

"Now I know I'm not the only one who hears the bell ringing like crazy," I yelled as I scurried down the stairs in the dark. I was still tying my red terry cloth robe with one hand and groping the wall for the light switch with the other when I asked who was at the door. "It's me Ang," Dorothy whispered.

I didn't have to even ask why she was here at 3 in the morning. I sighed as I unlocked the door, wondering what I'd find when I opened it. Would it be a black eye this time, a gaping wound or broken ribs? Dorothy had sustained all of them before and each time she showed up crying at my doorstep; leaving me to perform an amateur check up, guessing her diagnosis and rushing her to the emergency room. I was tired of reliving the same scene over and over again. It was like a low budget movie with a redundant plot. If Dorothy wasn't the sweetest person I had ever met, I would've surely given up on her years ago.

"Oh, Lord," I cried loudly as I looked at her. Here I was with absolutely no faith, crying out to somebody else's Savior. Dorothy came in.

"Sh, Ang. I don't want anyone to know about this…uh, it was an accident."

"Dorothy, you could go underground until this time next month and people would still see the bruises on your face," I lowered my voice until it matched hers, " What kind of accident could've possibly left you looking like this? Oh, I know, Glen accidently beat you senseless. I should..."

"Wait, it's not even like that. It's my fault. I was kind of flirting with this guy tonight at his friend's party. Glen loves me and he just gets real jealous. I was disrespecting him. When we got home, we got into this big fight and I hit him first.-he was just defending himself, really," Dorothy said sincerely.

"Tell yourself that story one hundred times Dorothy or however many times you need to in order to convince yourself `cause you'll never convince me. I'm going to get some ice. Maybe that'll help."

Dorothy was almost unrecognizable. One side of her face was red and blue and swollen. Her eyes were almost swollen shut and blood trickled from her nose and mouth. I knew all of my sisters well but I probably knew Dorothy the best. She's a very passive young lady but highly intelligent and compassionate. She'd probably give the shirt off of her back to anyone who needed it. I don't know how she became so nice, especially growing up with Billie. However, she didn't escape 'the curse'. We all struggled with some weakness because of our relation to Billie. Dorothy had always suffered from low self-esteem. She never saw herself as valuable. Even as a little girl, she thought she was nothing. She'd always say she couldn't do something-without even trying. We'd jump rope and ask her to jump in and she'd say, "I can't."

"Jackie's so pretty," she'd say, "Brandy is so confident and you and Rosa are the smartest people I know." She'd even find something nice to say about Gina. "And what about you," I'd ask. "Oh, I'm nothing special," she'd respond, "I'm just Dorothy." The worst thing about her comments were, that besides lacking Brandy's confidence, she had the rest of us beat. Dorothy is by far the prettiest, smartest, kindest person I've ever encountered.

She never dated in high school. Most of the guys were too intimidated to ask her out because she was so pretty. They all figured she was out of their league and most assumed she must have a boyfriend somewhere. She didn't have many girlfriends for the same reasons. Most of the girls were intimidated too. They were jealous of her looks and a lot of them thought she was conceited because she kept to herself. So when she met Glen her junior year, she was head over heels in a week. He was a popular senior who bathed her in compliments. Glen was a 6'8" star basketball player and when he began loving Dorothy, everyone else at school did too. She became the most popular girl in her school almost overnight. Maybe he beat her from the beginning, but I never saw any signs of it. I didn't get worried until after he graduated. Glen was a NBA hopeful. Two months before graduation, he sustained a knee injury and the doctors told him he had to give the sport up. Everyone had expected him to be drafted and when he wasn't, he was humiliated. The week after his graduation marks the anniversary of Dorothy's first black eye. Somehow, it was her fault that he hadn't achieved his goal. He talked Dorothy into moving in with him and having his baby. When she got pregnant, he told her it wasn't healthy for her to go to school everyday so Dorothy dropped out her senior year. No one knows why, but Dorothy miscarried. We all have our speculations. Things got worse for her after that. I've tried to talk her into getting her GED and going to college, but he forbids it. "You don't need all that, you've got me. I take good care of you. What, you don't think I'm enough? I'm not good enough for you, huh," he screamed when she had asked him about it. His tirade was followed by yet another beating.

He has threatened me several times. He scared off all of Dorothy's other friends, but I told him, I'm her sister, I'm here for life. Only a punk would hit a woman and Glen knows I'm not scared of him. I'll break him off a little something he'll never forget. He knows, that's why he'd never touch me.

"Dorothy, this ice doesn't even seem like it's helping."

"Ow," she screamed as I rubbed the washcloth full of ice cubes across her face.

"Please, don't let him keep doing this to you. You don't have to go back there…ever. You can stay here with me. Please, please, please," I begged.

Tears escaped from her puffy bruised eyes as she refused to even consider my words. "Let's just go to bed, o.k. Ang?" I told her I'd shut-up, but only if she promised to listen to me in the morning. She promised, as I put my arm around her and led her to my room.

"Oh my God, what happened to you," Jackie yelled as Dorothy

entered the kitchen, "It looks like you've been hit by a Mack truck."

"Shut-up Jackie, she still looks better than you on your best day," I groaned. Cruelty becomes me, I thought.

Billie rushed over to Dorothy and made her sit down. I could even see tears in her eyes.

"Baby, you grown. You goin' do what you want to do, but I'm going to tell you anyway. Get out...while you can."

In my twenty-nine years of existence, I've never heard Billie give any of her children sound advice, until now.

Jackie went on, "If she wants to let some man beat up on her, let her. It's her prerogative. Some women like that crazy stuff. All I know is, I would never let a man lay a finger on me, especially some okey dokey broke behind man."

"That's enough Jackie," I said. My tone must've been more powerful than usual or maybe Jackie realized she now lived in my house and I could throw her trampy butt in the street any time I felt like it. Where would she put her Mikasa then? Whatever the reason, she was silent.

After breakfast, Dorothy went upstairs with me, following close behind her. Sitting on my unmade bed, she gazed into the mirror which faced it. I plopped down on my tan flannel sheets and matching paisley comforter. We both sat in silence. Dorothy's face was still bruised and now it seemed to be puffier. You couldn't tell by looking at her now, but out of all of the girls, she looked the most like Billie. Jackie and Dorothy had Billie's fair skin, but Dorothy shared more than that. Her big, brown, almond-shaped eyes, her high cheekbones and thin, slightly pointed nose mirrored Billie's. The texture of her hair was even identical to our mother's. I always teased her because she didn't have to go through the tedious task of perming her hair every six weeks. As a matter of fact, Dorothy didn't put any effort into the upkeep of her hair. She simply brushed it all back and put it in a ponytail-and she was still beautiful. I imagine Billie would've looked like her if she hadn't taken up drinking. She tried to drink her cares away, but instead drank her looks away. Don't get me wrong, Billie still isn't an ugly woman, but all that remains of the beauty that could've been is a hardened shell.

Dorothy took a brush off of my dresser and returned to her prior position on the bed. She tugged at the rumpled scrunchie that was merely hanging by a few strands of her hair and began brushing her hair back. "You know you can't go back," I said, interrupting the silence that had enveloped us. Dorothy looked a little startled by my sudden outburst.

"You don't understand. None of you do. You don't know Glen like I do. He really loves me."

"So what you're telling me is that you're happy with him? The way things are, that's just fine with you?"

With those words spoken, Dorothy began to cry. It was as if my words hurt her more than the bruises.

"I want him to change," she sobbed, "Sometimes, he can be the sweetest man alive. A couple weeks ago, I woke up and he had prepared a picnic on the living room floor. It was perfect. I wish things could always be like that."

The whole thing sounded sweet but the truth of the matter is, Glen probably prepared the picnic to apologize for beating her the night before. I wanted to believe otherwise, but the history he and my sister shared prevented that.

"And what if he doesn't change Dorothy? What then? Are you going to sacrifice your physical and mental health waiting to see if your wish will come true? "

Dorothy didn't answer.

"What if he doesn't change, Dorothy?" I repeated.

She sat there looking down at the floor as if she was pondering the most profound thought.

"He will," she whispered.

CHAPTER 11

NANA, THE NEIGHBORHOOD WATCHMAN

Old Ms. Johnson. She was a feisty old woman who always wore her blue-gray hair in a bun and her cat-eyed glasses on a chain around her neck. I had never looked in her closet but I'd swear she owned a sweat suit in every color of the rainbow. Every time I saw Dorothy's neighbor, she was wearing a different color sweat suit, some tube socks and a pair of moccasins. As if she wasn't eccentric enough, she always spoke in the form of a question. She'd say, "It's a lovely day, ain't that right?" So it always took her twice as long to get a point across. Conversing with her, I felt like a contestant on the ghetto rendition of Jeopardy. Even though she was older, she had full control of all of her faculties. She knew everything that happened in Dorothy's apartment building and didn't mind sharing the information. At first I just saw her as a nosy old lady, but Dorothy tried to get me to think differently. She thought highly of the elderly woman. Dorothy brought her meals, accompanied her on outings and always bought her a gift for her birthday and Christmas. The more I went to visit my sister, the better I got to know Ms. Johnson and I begun to realize that she was just a lonely lady in need of companionship. I'd knock on my sister's door, turn around and I'd see her beady little eyes peering out of a crack in the door. It wasn't long before she began inviting me into her home to sit down and watch whichever game show or soap opera she happened to be tuning into. She'd fill me in on what was going on between Glen and Dorothy and all of her surrounding neighbors. Eventually, I stopped visiting my sister so my visits with Ms. Johnson ceased also. Dorothy had begged me not to stop coming by but I couldn't take hearing about the repercussions she suffered because of my visits. During my last visit, I gave Ms. Johnson my address and phone number. I told her to call me if things ever got out of hand. She seemed honored to have been given the trusted role and assured me that she'd call if anything warranted it.

Needless to say, I used to speak to the old woman weekly. Those times when Dorothy didn't end up at my house, I was still aware of what was going on in her life. I heard about the bangs and the crashes and the screaming that occurred in her apartment. When I realized Dorothy was not going to ever leave Glen, I stripped my elderly friend of her neighborhood watch badge. I told Ms. Johnson that we could continue our phone conversations, but it was no longer necessary for her to update me on my sister's home life, especially since Dorothy ended up at my door ninety percent of the time anyway. We still talk and upon her request, I've given her the honorary title "Nana". I've never let Dorothy in on me and Nana's secret. She was just thrilled that we became friends. "She has no family, well, not really. She needs people to care about her," my sister had encouraged me. Then she uttered her favorite saying. Every time my siblings argued, every time Billie angered one of us, if Dorothy was around, she would find her way over to the offended parties, wrap her arm around them and say, "We've got to love each other. If we don't, who will?" Dorothy's love for Ms. Johnson led her to visit nursing homes. She said it hurt her to think that there were thousands of Ms. Johnsons everywhere. When Nana heard about Dorothy's latest cause, she said what she always said whenever my sister's name was even mentioned, "She's a special lady, ain't that right?" Yes, a special lady indeed.

CHAPTER 12

IGNORANCE IS BLISS

"What a rough day," I let out in a loud sigh as I opened the door, my keys and the mail in one hand while I struggled to hold a pizza and my briefcase in the other arm. "People can't even help out and get the mail around here. How long does that take," I said aloud, obviously agitated, as I laid the pizza on the kitchen counter. I headed straight for the living room and the couch, throwing my briefcase down along the way. The plastic crinkled as I sat down. I had bought the burgundy and creme sofa just before Billie invited Gina's kids to stay. Needless to say, I vowed to never remove the plastic. Taking my brown pumps off, I put my stocking feet up on the mahogany coffee table. I usually forbade everyone from putting their feet up on the furniture but tonight I was breaking one of my own rules, and it felt good.

Jackie came running down the stairs. Judging from her 'hooker wear', she must have a date, I thought. Since she and Bob broke up, she had been on several dates but she always came home complaining. Somehow, the guy had misrepresented himself and allowed her to believe he was worth a lot more than he truly was. She'd come home, slam the door and yell, "He couldn't afford me!" That did not stop her though, she was convinced to find a new sugar daddy. "I thought I heard Angela's voice," Jackie said, as she stood at the bottom of the stairs in a slinky scarlet dress that ended about four inches before her knee began. I should pretend I'm not here, I thought as I sat in the pitch black room, but my mouth betrayed me.

"I'm in here Jackie, what do you want?"

"Oh, I didn't even see you. Why are you sitting in the dark? Never mind. I want to borrow that bright red lipstick you had on the other day. All of my reds are too dull for this dress," Jackie said, brushing the cascading curls out of her face.

You can't borrow my lipstick; I don't know where your lips have been, I thought, but instead I asked, "You've got a hot date?" Knowing how Jackie feels about me I figure she must've been dying to tell someone, anyone, about this new guy she's seeing because she didn't give me her usual response-"none of your business".

"Well, he may be worth seeing," she said, "He manages a few rap groups and he drives a Benz. That is, if he's not being driven around in his limo. He's got a condo in New York, a home in Florida and a home in California. It's a start."

"The lipstick is right on my dresser. It's called fiery passion," I said, "You can have it."

I have another one that's similar, I thought, reassuring myself. Shoot, I don't want it after she's used it, and with that thought, I laid my head back on the plastic. Without uttering another word, Jackie turned around and skipped up the stairs. What, I said to myself, no mention of this guy's nice personality and I giggled out loud.

Darn, I must've dozed off. I had just been startled by the slamming of the front door. I wanted to see what this new boyfriend of Jackie's looked like. Oh well, it's not likely that he came to the door anyway. Jackie has been places and done things I've only dreamed about and yet she still runs out of the house when a man honks his horn. No class, I said to myself.

I got up from the couch, picked up my shoes, my briefcase and headed up the stairs. I could hear the kids wrestling around downstairs as Billie laughed. What a mother she is to those kids, I thought, well, I guess, better late than never.

2 a.m. and I haven't been to sleep yet. I had been so tired earlier. I was skulking down the stairs on my way to the kitchen to get some ice cream when I saw the front door ajar. Putting my insomnia behind me, I ran down the remaining steps. When I went to shut the door, Brandy, who was standing on the other side, let out a holler.

"Hey, hey, wait a minute, let me in he..he..her..this place," she said.

"How long have you been standing there," I asked, "And why didn't you just come in the house?"

Before she could even begin to answer my questions, I smelled the liquor on her breath. It was so strong, I felt like I was getting a contact high.

"LLL...look, I..I...I don't have to say nothing...to you. You ain't my mama...or my man-now you get out my way."

With those words, Brandy stretched out her hand as if to push me and ended up falling on her face.

"So this is what you've been doing all these weeks? Feeling sorry for yourself? Staying out late, drinking?" I dared to ask another question after her rebuke. "Don't even bother answering," I said, disgusted, as I lifted Brandy to her feet and practically carried her up the stairs.

I took off her coat and her shoes and laid her across her bed. As I stood in the doorway, I began to have flashbacks of the many weekends I had put Billie to bed when she, too, came home too inebriated to even stand. I will not live through this again, I said out loud. Deep down within myself, I knew I wouldn't survive it a second time.

Now it was 2 p.m. and as I sat in the small, cramped office, I began to have second thoughts. Maybe I shouldn't be here. No, I know I shouldn't, I thought. Why did I always do this? I always found myself trying to fix everybody's problems, even when they seemed absolutely unfixable. What would this solve, I asked myself. Too late, I can't get up and leave now, I thought, as the door of the office opened and in stepped a tall lanky white woman dressed conservatively in a blue pin striped suit. "Hi, how are you," she asked as she took her place behind the cluttered wooden desk. What had possessed me to call Brandy's former supervisor and schedule a meeting? Did I really think I could get her job back? I guess I was hoping I could and then maybe she'd go back to being her old self. I had dreamed of being greeted with apologies as Gloria Rizzo, Brandy's boss, explained that her lay off was temporary and how she'd be getting a call asking her to return any day.

"Fine, and you?" I responded, feigning a smile.

"So what is it that you've come to see me about...Ms. Roberts," Ms. Rizzo asked looking down at her desk calendar.

"I'm Brandy Roberts' sister," I said.

"Oh," she interrupted.

"I understand that Brandy was laid off and I just wanted to know how long the lay off might last. I was told that no information could be given out over the phone, that's when I scheduled this appointment with you," I said in my most sincere and proper voice.

"There must be some kind of misunderstanding," the woman said nervously.

I knew it, I thought. Brandy has been such a hard worker for so long, I knew it would only be a matter of time before they asked her back.

"Brandy Roberts was terminated."

There was that brick again! This time I had heard it from the horse's mouth.

"Terminated? May I ask why?"

The supervisor began to explain that it was against policy to disclose such personal information unless the request was coming from a potential employer checking references. I have always been thought of as a strong person by family and peers. I rarely cry and when I do, I make sure I'm all alone. So it was just as shocking to me as it was to Ms. Rizzo when I burst into tears in her office. I wasn't even embarrassed by my inappropriate emotional display. I'd never see this white lady again, I thought. What was more surprising than my tears were my words. I began to explain to this woman how I am the caretaker of my entire family; how I knew Brandy needed me but I couldn't help her until I knew why she had been fired from a job, in which she once had such pride. Ms. Rizzo obviously felt sorry for me because she agreed to tell me everything as she handed me a box of Kleenex.

What followed was a conversation which I shall never forget. I'd seen friends of accused serial killers on the news saying how kind the person was and how shocked they were to discover that this person was a mass murderer. I remember listening to such testimonies in disbelief. How could anyone be so clueless about someone they called neighbor or friend? Hadn't they noticed people going into Jeffrey Dahmer's home and wondered why they had never seen them leave? Now, here I sat listening to some woman tell me about my sister... but the person she described was someone else. How long had Brandy been living this double life? I sat, shocked, as Ms. Rizzo proceeded to tell me how my sister had gone from a diligent employee working her way through the ranks to a rowdy drunk working her way through the nearby bars. She said Brandy made a habit of coming back from lunch intoxicated, and though she had been warned several times, her destructive behavior did not cease.

"It hurt my heart to have to let her go. Brandy seemed to be something special," Ms. Rizzo continued, staring down at her desk, "I even brought her in here a few times and tried to get her to open up and maybe get at the source of the drinking, but nothing. She'd always say she only had a couple drinks. Her performance said otherwise."

Ms. Rizzo, who was once reluctant to speak to me, would not stop talking now. I guess she could not tell by the expression on my face that I had heard enough. What had begun as an explanation was slowly becoming an opportunity for her to exercise her hobby, which must've been amateur psychology. I could no longer listen to her ramble on and on about how Brandy's environment may have led to her occupational demise or perhaps, those with whom she spent her time were to blame.

I could no longer stomach Ms. Rizzo's unwanted analysis and lingering assumptions. Staring at this blue-eyed, blonde-haired woman, I no longer saw her as my ally. The only thing left out of her ramblings were the words, "you people". My rage flourished. How could Brandy do this? Not only bring shame to herself and her family, but every black person who is striving to prove themselves everyday. Some people expect us to act like fools, I thought, how could she give them fuel to keep on believing the stereotypes? My ears were ringing and I felt like I was turning red-no small feat for a chocolate woman like myself. I got up and left. I didn't thank Ms. Rizzo for her time; I didn't say goodbye or nice meeting you or any other phony nicety. I just picked my purse up, got up out of the chair and walked out. Why bother being polite, I thought; why the heck should I give a darn what she thinks of me? She already knows my sister is a drunk.

Outside of the office, I stopped some lady and asked her where the restroom was. I was physically sick. I could not stop bawling as I got on my knees and hugged the toilet as if it were my own. Giving no thought to life-threatening germs or bacteria that may be living in the stall or on the seat, I vomited. I was trying to purge my soul, but all that surfaced was my lunch.

CHAPTER 13

EPIPHANY

Driving home on 287, I had to convince myself, more than once, not to slam into a semi-truck or just simply let go of the wheel and allow the car to move as it pleased. My life had always been out of control-why shouldn't it end the same way? I had been driving around for a long time thinking before I finally decided to head home. "Isn't this a trip?" I yelled. These were the first words I had spoken in over an hour. "My sister is a drunk and I'm contemplating suicide." Billie and my sisters have brought me nothing but pain and now instead of sharing my home with a wonderful husband, I'm sharing it with them. "My home is filled with nothing, but reminders of how painful my life has been," I said aloud. Although I was tempted to try to cheer myself up with the words, "it could be worse", I dared not think it or say it. I knew from experience that things not only could, but would do exactly that.

I needed someone to talk to-anyone, so I could stop talking to myself. After all, it was getting me nowhere. It seemed like I had always been and would always be the backbone for everyone and I no longer wanted the job. Who could I lean on in my time of need? Sure, I have a few friends, even a couple with whom I work, but I never shared these kinds of things with them. I hadn't spoken to my best friend Tammy in over a month because I was too busy trying to maintain my sanity. I was too embarrassed to let her or anyone else in on the joke that was my life. I was too ashamed to let anyone in my world. If I did, they'd know that everything and everyone around me was dysfunctional. I guess in a lot of ways, I, like Brandy, was living a dual existence. I am a facade. To the outside world, I'm strong, confident, I've got it all together, but inside I am the same weak child seeking out a love and acceptance I'll probably never obtain.

I should give Rosa a call, I thought. She knows me better than anyone, but I know she moved all the way to California to get away from this cancer, called family. Not only that, Rosa and I had changed a lot over the years. Rosa met her husband at Stanford and even though she earned a bachelor's degree, she's never used it. She stays at home with her daughter, Brianna. Her husband, Bryan, thinks that her parents are dead and that if it wasn't for me, she'd be an only child.

Rosa took walks in the park, went camping with her husband and her daughter and planned dinner parties. I was grateful for those times when I could find a dark empty corner of the house in which to retreat. The only glimpse I got of a park was of the one I passed on my way to work every morning. Rosa's biggest gripe was that she couldn't find the perfect bag to go with the Jones New York pantsuit Bryan had recently purchased for her. While each day I worked about 10 hours doing a job, for which I had no zeal, just to keep on top of my bills and put food into the six mouths that did not belong to me. Needless to say, Rosa's blues were not my blues. Serves me right for sticking around!

As I pulled into the driveway, I moved my rearview mirror and glanced in it. I tried to wipe away any evidence that I had been crying. I decided I would not confront Brandy. "Wimp," I said, looking at my reflection. Brandy would have to go though. It was obvious now that she had a problem and she had not been looking for work. She could forget getting a good recommendation from the post office-the only job she ever had. With just a high school diploma, her future was limited, but being a closet alcoholic made it completely dim. She'd have to go. Sooner or later, I thought.

As I walked through the door, I heard screaming. Another terrific greeting after a long hard day.

"Look, don't be getting all jealous just because your sorry butt can't find a man… 'cause you a sorry poor-excuse for a woman. All these nappy heads running around here and ain't none of them got the same daddy," Jackie hollered.

"You know what Jackie? You ain't even got to go there. I was just trying to look out for you…never again," Gina paused, "And you may think I'm a ho, but at least I've had feelings for every man I've laid down with. You lay down and come up completely numb, you coldhearted bi-"

Before Gina could finish, I ran in and interrupted, "What's going on in here? What's all the yelling about?"

"The police have arrived," Jackie snorted, leaving the room as if I hadn't asked a question.

"I told them to just drop it," Billie said nonchalantly as she and Gina's kids sat at the table eating potato chips.

"Billie, take the kids downstairs please. They shouldn't be up here witnessing this chaos," I said.

I started to ask her why she didn't realize that on her own, but then I realized to whom I was talking. I continued, "Gina, I don't care what you and Jackie were fighting about, you shouldn't be letting your kids watch. Do you want them to end up as messed up as the rest of us?"

Gina, who was now crying, told me that she had come over to warn Jackie about some guy she had started seeing. She said one of her girlfriends had an aunt who had been "played" by him. So, I thought, let Jackie get played, as long as she gets some money out of him first she won't care. "You don't understand," Gina said, "This Daryl, he puts on this front like he's some big time producer, but he ain't nothing but a drug dealer…and a pimp." Pimp? Gina had succeeded in taking my mind off of my pity party. She had my undivided attention now. Even after the Women's Liberation Movement, there were still women who gave all of their money to a man?

"Jackie thinks she's so tough," Gina continued, still crying, "But she doesn't know who she's messing with. There's no telling what she could get herself into."

"It's her life Gina," I finally responded, "If she wants to screw it up; if she wants to date a pimp or whoever, that's her prerogative...and you know it's a funny thing, but I think he is the one we should be warning. Jackie can take care of herself."

CHAPTER 14

ANYWHERE BUT HOME

I never thought I'd look forward to getting out of my warm comfortable bed, peeling my head from my down pillow to head off to work, but life is full of surprises. I didn't sleep well last night. I kept tossing and turning, thinking about the turmoil that is my life. I figure going to work will take my mind off of everything. After all, brokers have never failed to keep me busy. Their only purpose was to represent the clients and they relished their responsibility. They were constantly calling me, asking me to change this or that in a policy. At work, I rarely have time to think about anything other than business, which suits me just fine today.

The day must've had wings because it simply flew by. It's just my luck that the one day I'm actually happy to be here goes by with ease. I must admit I had a great day. I wrote a $200,000 account-another big dent in the book of business I was given at the beginning of the year. If I keep going at this rate, I'll reach my million dollar written premium goal in no time.

"Hey Angela. Real busy today, huh?"

I hadn't even heard Belinda approach my cubicle, "Yeah, girl, I came to work today," I said smiling. I had been feigning grins all day, keeping up the facade of strong confident happy Angela, but this smile was genuine.

Belinda was a very nice person. Everyone knew she was a God-fearing woman with a lot of class and a big heart. She was the person who remembered everybody's birthday and bought a card. She'd even buy cards for the janitor and people who worked in the mailroom. When she passed the cards around, we'd all sign our names in bright red ink, pretending to be thoughtful. Although she was nice, what I respected most about her was that she didn't allow herself to be anyone's doormat. She was extremely good at her job and she let the managers know that she knew her worth-not an easy task in Corporate America.

I remember when she was promoted from a Senior Underwriter to Marketing Manager. Some people were quite agitated. She had only been the third black promoted to management in the branch and she was new to the company. We were having lunch shortly after her promotion, which we often did, when two women sitting at an adjacent table interrupted our conversation to congratulate her. One of the women had also been a candidate for the job. She said how surprising it was that Belinda had received it. She kept repeating, "Oh, you must be thrilled, you must feel so lucky." After the third repetition, I grew weary of the woman. Belinda, with a loving smile that I still believe to this day was sincere, finally responded, "Yes, I feel blessed. I am very excited about the opportunity, especially since I know it was merit and not luck that helped me secure the position… and what exactly shocked you? Was it the fact that I'm black or that I've acquired twice the business you have in the seven months that I've been here?" The woman turned red and begun apologizing profusely. She did not mean to imply anything negative, she claimed. I wanted to double over in laughter, but I managed to keep my composure. Belinda accepted the woman's apology, that smile never once departing her face. The woman, Susan, to whom she had been speaking, was known for belittling people in the workplace and always had something sarcastic to say. Looking at Belinda's face, I knew, and so did Susan, that she had not spoken out of malice. She wasn't trying to get revenge for all those who had been slain, at one time or another, by Susan's tongue. She was simply speaking her mind. Now, she was standing at my desk trying to find out how I was doing as she so often did.

"So everything's good right?" Belinda asked.

"Couldn't be better," I said with a grin, hoping she wouldn't see through the lie.

"Well, I don't know if you'd be up for a night on the town tonight, but I just wanted to invite you to my church. We're having a revival all this week," she explained, "If you decide to come out, just let me know. I can either pick you up or give you directions."

No,No,No, not church, I thought. She had me going for a while, talking about 'a night on the town'. I don't want to go home, but I don't think I'm willing to go to church just to avoid it.

"Uh, maybe, Belinda I don't know. I'll let you know."

She seemed to anticipate the reaction I gave. Laughing she said, "Do that." I had gathered all of my belongings and logged off of my computer. I had purposely loaded my briefcase with files. I had made up my mind that upon arriving home, I would put on my pajamas, get a huge bowl of ice cream and climb in bed with my files. Shoot, who needs dinner when there's good ol' butter pecan in the freezer? When my eyes could no longer focus on the paperwork and my ice cream was devoured, I'd turn in for the night. My mind had come up with the plan and I thought all of my body parts agreed, so I was just as surprised as Belinda when I found myself in her office asking for directions to the church. I immediately tried to explain my shocking behavior, moreso to myself than to Belinda, rationalizing what seemed to me, to be irrational behavior.

"I may come one night...um, uh, just in case I do, I'd rather get directions now, so I won't have to bother you later," I explained.

I got into my car, put the key into the ignition and sat staring into space. All I could think of was the tremendous stress I had been feeling lately and the overwhelming dread I felt about returning home. I looked over the directions Belinda had given me. I know where this is, I thought, sometimes I pass it on my way to Uncle Jack's Rib Shack. What the heck, I thought, it sure can't hurt. It may even make me feel better. If I remember correctly, some of those church women can have some humorous shouts. Although I hadn't been inside a church since my grandparents' funeral, in my mind I could still see the women swallowed up by large hats, running up and down the aisles, arms flailing, feet shuffling. What a show! That's just what I need tonight, some entertainment, I said to myself.

I pulled into the parking lot of the church. It was filling fast. As I studied the lot looking for a space to pull my leased maroon Volvo into, I noticed how eager the people getting out of their cars looked. Some of them almost appeared to be giddy as they drew nearer to the church entrance. It's not too late to go home, I thought. It's not like I know anyone here, except Belinda and she hasn't seen me yet. My mind seemed to be thinking a mile a minute, but my body wasn't listening. Despite my reluctance, I was putting the club on my car. Before opening my car door, I looked in the rearview mirror to check my makeup. I should've spent a little extra money and got a car with a driver's side mirror, I thought. I got out of my car. As I walked through the parking lot, I was greeted by smiling faces. I returned the gesture, wondering if they were just being kind or if I had something hanging out of my nose. I have always grown paranoid as I enter a church. As I approached the doors, I suddenly remembered what else plagued me when I went to church-butterflies. My stomach was doing a dance. I hoped this wasn't one of those churches where the people frowned upon women wearing pants, lipstick and the color red, especially since I happened to be wearing a red pantsuit with matching red lipstick. In my grandma's church I would've been considered a 'sure 'nuf sinner'.

"Welcome to Greater Love church," said a friendly elderly woman wearing a black and white dress. "I hope you enjoy the service," she continued as she handed me a program which outlined the week's events. "Thank you," I responded cheerfully. She must be an usher, I thought as I spotted five other women adorned in the same colors, also greeting people who entered. I made my way into the sanctuary. People were rushing in as if they were being seated for a concert. I didn't have to look around for the perfect seat. I plopped down in the very last pew. When I was little, I'd always feel bad for that poor unsuspecting visitor who came to a service sophisticated and polished and then ended up falling out "in the Spirit", as my grandmother put it, or running around the church. How embarrassing, I used to think. Back here I should be out of the reach of the Holy Spirit, I thought. The church filled up quickly and pretty soon people were clamoring for seats next to me. I accommodated them but I made sure that I kept my seat at the end of the pew so I could be close to the door in case I needed to make a fast exit; like once the preacher made an altar call-asking those in need of prayer to come up to the front or if they made the visitors stand and say something. What would I possibly say? "Hi, my name is Angela Roberts. I don't go to church. Actually, I don't really believe in all of this, but anywhere is better than home tonight." I'd rather die than get up and speak in front of all of these strangers.

The organist began playing and the congregation joined together in song. A mighty fine organist, I might add. People began rocking and swaying, and pew by pew, they began to stand with tear-filled eyes and hands raised. I wasn't paying attention to the words in the song, I was too busy scanning the audience to see if I could find Belinda in the massive crowd. Wow, there's a lot of men here, I thought. My grandparent's church had been predominantly women. "I didn't know so many men went to church," I whispered, not even realizing I had spoken aloud. A young woman sitting next to me must've thought the comment was directed to her because she interrupted my thoughts.

"I was surprised too the first time I came, but girl, the Lord died for everyone. It's about time men are starting to see that."

I just smiled in response, even though I wanted to say, "I wasn't even talking to you." I'll let her feel good about herself, thinking she's educated somebody, I thought, this time silently. Hallelujahs and Thank you Jesus-es filled the atmosphere as I questioned myself once more. What am I doing here, I asked myself as I fought back a yawn.

At that moment, a fat, short man dressed in a brown suit stood before the congregation. He read some scripture about giving and as he gave his testimony, the ushers proceeded down the aisles, passing the collection baskets. Oh, I knew there would be an offering, I thought, as I shuffled through my wallet looking for a dollar bill. The man was explaining how he used to refuse to give an offering to the church. He said he always paid tithes and figured that was enough. Only after he began to "search the scriptures", as he put it, did he realize he was blocking his blessings. "Give and it shall be given back to you," he continued. "Amen" began to echo through the building. I better give more, I thought, feeling a little guilty. So I pulled two more dollars out of my pocketbook. That should do it, I said to myself. "Show God that you trust him enough to give and I promise you he'll return it to you double-fold," the man shouted smiling. The congregation began to sing a song that I had never heard before and the words were almost identical to those spoken by the fat man. "Give and he'll give it back to you, Give and he'll give it back to you, pressed down, shaken together, running over...he'll give it back to you." This is doing nothing for me, I thought, perhaps, this would be the perfect time to make my getaway. Then, suddenly the audience stood and a short, caramel-colored woman donning a kinte cloth headwrap entered the pulpit. She didn't waste time getting to the point. At my grandparents' church, I remember there had always been a lot of singing and announcements before the preacher came forth. Elder Smith instructed everyone to open their bibles to the book of Psalms and she read from the 127th chapter. "Unless the Lord builds the house," she began, "they labor in vain, who build it. Unless the Lord guards the city, the watchman stays awake in vain. It is vain for you to rise up early, to sit up late..." Completing the scripture and closing her bible, she continued, "My text tonight is, 'If the Lord doesn't do it, it can't be done.' There are people in here tonight who are tired, discouraged and those who are downtrodden by life. You're so overwhelmed by your circumstances that you can't see past them. You're trying to handle things on your own, but why? Why? When the Lord said in his Word that we can cast our cares upon him. I'm telling you, you can keep on trying to make it on your own but you may go crazy trying. You can work hard, do all you know to do, but unless you lean on the Lord, all you do will be in vain. Don't live a vain life!"

As the Elder spoke, I kept looking around to see if anyone else was feeling as violated as I was. It was like this woman had placed hidden cameras in my home. She pinpointed how I was feeling and what I was going through. I didn't know whether to squat down and leave the building in shame or stand up so I could see her better. When she had finished her sermon, people were shouting and the choir began singing. I decided to leave before the preacher came out and called me by name. I had almost reached the door when I heard Belinda's voice.

"Angela, wait, wait one minute."

"How did you see me with all of these people here," I asked.

"I guess I just looked up at the right moment"

Belinda thanked me for coming. "I'm not going to put you on the spot right now, but we'll talk," she said.

I laughed. "I know we will," I replied as I pushed the big wooden church doors open and exited the church.

As I drove home the words, "labor in vain" kept reverberating through my mind. "In vain," I said aloud as I pulled into the drive-way.

CHAPTER 15

SOLD OUT

It's been three weeks since I visited Belinda's church, but I can't get the preacher's message out of my head. I can't shake the feeling that she was talking to me. After all, no matter how hard I try, it seems like my actions are futile. Sometimes, I wonder why I even bother. There is however, a silver lining to every dark cloud. My boss just informed me that after a thorough evaluation, he's decided to give me a raise. I could always use more money even though I have to admit, I've been doing a pretty good job saving money, in spite of my many responsibilities. I recently added Brandy's car note to my stack of bills. If she's going to look for a job, she needs a car, right? "I've been thinking about taking a little vacation …maybe five days in the Caribbean alone would do me some good. I can feel the sunlight beaming on my head now. I can taste the pina colada with the little umbrella floating along the side of the glass. I can feel the warm sand between my toes. Yeah, I think I will take that vacation. I'll call a travel agent tomorrow.

Something strange is going on. Jackie was up early this morning, skipping around the house like a schoolgirl. It is extremely unusual to see her face before noon on Saturday. She left the house in typical weekend gear- a creme bodysuit and a pair of tight blue Bill Blass jeans. When she returned home a few hours later she had a woman with her. She did not look like she belonged in Jackie's crowd. She was an older woman and didn't appear to be a hoochie.

Even though I appeared to be engulfed in my housework, I couldn't help being nosy. The woman smiled at me as she waited in the doorway, trying to hide her obvious discomfort.

Jackie returned to the doorway carrying a bag, looked at me suspiciously and escorted the stranger outside. "Goodbye," I shouted to the lady as Jackie slammed the door behind her. I glanced out of the bay window in front of the house and saw Jackie give the woman the gold gift bag in exchange for what appeared to be money. The woman then got into her white Toyota Corolla and drove away. Jackie hopped into her navy blue luxury car and did the same. "I don't know what she's up to," I said to myself, "but it can't be good."

Evening came quickly but I didn't care. "Angie," Billie called, "I think you should come down here." I had heard the doorbell, but decided to ignore it since no one ever came to see me.

Lately, I have completely withdrawn from the family. While my weekends used to be spent taking my niece and nephews to Sportsworld or some other game-filled romper room, I had spent the last couple in my room with the door shut. It was the closest thing I had to a retreat. I booked my vacation for next month so I had to do something to keep my sanity in the meantime. I felt so guilty when Wadell, my nephew, came to my door asking me if he and his siblings had done something wrong. It was quite difficult trying to explain to a 7-year-old that I need "me" time. When the conversation ended, I had promised to take them to a matinee tomorrow. I pampered myself all day, indulging in two bubble baths. I even gave myself a manicure and a pedicure as I tuned into the Twilight Zone marathon. I had managed to spend the entire day in the tranquility of my room, only exiting to get another donut, an extra scoop of ice cream, a bag of chips or some other fat-filled, artery-clogging treat...until now.

"What's up Billie," I yelled, cracking my bedroom door to hear her response. I didn't want to have to leave my place of refuge now. "It's some guys down here with a U-haul truck." A what? I thought. Is someone moving out, I said to myself, with a glimmer of hope in my voice. I threw on my robe and headed downstairs. Before I could even ask what was going on, the young lady standing in my doorway spoke.

"I'm here to pick up the bed...the brass bed. Jackie told me I could come get it tonight."

"Oh, did she?" I asked, sarcasm dripping off of my tongue.

"Yes, she said I could take the frame as long as I left the mattress behind, which is just fine with me since I already have a mattress that'll fit the bed...and you know beds like that, I mean, what she sold it for, are just really hard to find. I mean..."

I realized that I had to cut this lady off or she'd still be talking this time tomorrow night. "I'll show you where it is," I said, interrupting. The two men standing behind her followed me up the stairs to the attic. Jackie hadn't even mentioned that she was selling her bed. She loved that bed. Nikki, the young lady, said she had learned about the bed from a flyer she saw hanging up in a local supermarket. She spoke to Jackie and earlier this week they met outside of that same market and Nikki had given my sister three hundred dollars. That's when Jackie told her she could pick it up anytime. The whole thing seemed weird to me, very weird.

I debated with myself all night whether I should ask Jackie for an explanation regarding her recent unusual behavior or whether I should just forget about it. Jackie was a grown woman who had proven she could get by on her own. It is difficult to imagine that she may be having money problems, especially considering the material gain she acquired while with Bob. However, she's never been the most responsible person. Perhaps, she's squandered her savings trying to live the same way she did when someone else was picking up the tab. It would be just like Jackie to be in trouble and never say anything. She'd probably rather die than accept any help from me. I'll give it some time, I thought, and if things continue to get stranger, I'll talk to her.

Jackie would kill me if she knew I was entering her room, I thought, as I tiptoed up the attic stairs. "I just want to look on her dresser to see if she took my mascara," I said to myself, justifying my deceit. Jackie has a habit of borrowing my makeup. As I scanned the oak dresser, a pile of receipts caught my eye. My conscience pleaded with me, reminding me that my sister deserved a certain amount of privacy but I ignored it and perused through the papers. The receipts were from pawn shops and each contained lists of jewelry. It seemed like Jackie was slowly selling everything she owned. My mind was made up. I had to find out what was going on.

"Please, don't say anything," Jackie cried, when I finally confronted her. Who was I going to tell? As if anyone but me even cared. "I had a lot of credit cards and "I used them all. When Bob ended it, I was left hanging. I've been handling it the best way I can."

It's true, Jackie and I don't get along but my heart is not so hardened that I can't feel sympathy for her. She was talking about selling some of her clothes next, her dresser and maybe, eventually her car. Now, since Jackie has been living with me, I haven't had to give her a dime. She has taken care of herself. Of course, she hasn't offered me a dime either...for groceries or rent. With that considered, it still wasn't long before I found myself searching for my checkbook.

"How much do you need to make things right Jackie," I asked.

"About a thousand dollars, but consider this a loan... not a handout. I'll pay you back, I swear."

As I signed the check, I couldn't help but think, there goes my vacation.

CHAPTER 16

DATELESS

I can't ever remember feeling this way. I can't ever recall giving much thought to my love life…the possibility of having one or the fact that mine was currently non-existent and had been that way for nearly a decade. I have only had one real relationship with a man, and the truth be told, he was just a boy. Tareek, some guy I met in college. Tall, nice looking and intelligent. He was extremely militant and headed the school's Black Student Union. Although our personalities were conflicting, my curiosity got the best of me and I decided to give it a try. It didn't work out because Tareek was the type of guy who always needed his ego stroked. He wanted someone who thought it was all about him. All his conversations were filled with ways he planned to start a new revolution. He was a Muslim and you would've thought he was going to be the next Malcolm X. He was always running around campus explaining how "our people" were oppressed. How black folks had to raise their level of awareness. Tareek, not only refrained from eating pork or wearing anything but a dashiki and black jeans, he had also given up his track scholarship because he said black men had to take their rightful place and stop running for and from "the man".

He was also the one I shared my first and only intimate experiences. I had no desire to have sex in high school because in my mind, after watching Billie, the only thing it was good for was having babies and who wants to have a kid at sixteen? Anyway,

Tareek wanted a woman who raised more than his consciousness. From the moment I met him, he was constantly trying to get in my pants. After we started dating for a while, I gave in to his advances. I don't know if it was his performance or just me, but the experience ended with my feelings still unchanged. Sex is highly overrated. Maybe Tareek picked up on my lack of enthusiasm after a few times because he eventually dumped me for another girl...a white girl! Oh, he claimed they had just been set up as partners for some class project. It became obvious to me that more was going on when I walked into his dorm room and caught the white girl getting out of the shower.

"You're not going to tell anyone about this... are you Angie? I mean, I've got a cause to think about," were the only words he spoke after he ran down the hall to catch me.

"You know me," I responded, "I don't hold grudges."

My friend Tammy and I made flyers with Tareek's number near the phrase 'for a good time, call' and passed them out outside some New York gay club. It was Tammy's idea, but I got a lot of satisfaction out of it. I don't know why, since I was actually relieved the relationship was over. I've always felt uncomfortable around men, awkward even.

That's why I'm so surprised that I've been thinking about Daniel, the church organist. I can't get him out of my mind. His over six- foot frame, his gorgeous hazel eyes. Both times I've visited Greater Love Fellowship church, he has greeted me with a wave and a grin as wide as the pulpit. I remember looking around as if to say, "are you talking to me?" He's probably nice to everyone who visits. After all, the entire congregation seems to be unusually friendly. I don't even know if he's married and I dare not ask Belinda. I don't want her to think I just visited her church to shop for a husband. Anyway, the last thing I need right now is a man in my life. I've been too busy trying to keep my family together to concentrate on dating. I have had a few successful dates in the past, but the men moved on after weeks of leaving unanswered messages on my voicemail. If that didn't turn them off then putting up with a series of canceled dates did. I'd have to bail out on them because I had to take Dorothy to the emergency room, counsel Gina, take

Billie here or there or pick one of the kids up from one extracurricular activity or another. If anyone ever did become interested in me enough to pursue a relationship, I'm sure he'd quickly change his mind after meeting my "loved ones". Who'd want to marry into a family as messed up as mine? I'm sure they wouldn't want my warped gene pool to even touch their family tree.

CHAPTER 17

A MONSTER IN THE ATTIC

I just can't seem to shake this headache and usually Tylenol works for me. A two-hour nap should help alleviate some of this pain, I thought, as I pulled into the driveway, right next to Jackie's car. In the seven years that I've worked for Franklin and Son, I can count the days I've called in sick on one hand. Today I had to leave early. It feels like rounds of gunfire are going off in my head. Bang! Bang! Bang! There it goes again.

More bills, I said to myself, as I shuffled through the mail, placing it in its usual spot on the kitchen counter.

"Billie, I'm home," I yelled down the basement stairs.

"Sh, sh," I heard her whisper as she approached the steps.

Leron and Jaquan must be napping, I thought. Billie stayed home during the week with my three and a half and two- year-old nephews while Laquesha and Wadell went to school around the corner.

"What you doing here," she asked as if she was concerned. The only concern she had was making sure I hadn't gotten fired because then her free ride would end.

"I'm a little sick, I came home to lay down"

This time there was no response. I hadn't expected any. I had been taking care of my own ailments ever since I stepped foot into Billie's home. She had always been too drunk to take out time to tend to stomachaches, headaches or even fevers. I had taken my sisters to the clinic whenever they were too ill to be treated at home. Thank God for Medicaid. Even now whenever her grandchildren get sick, Billie will approach me, hysterically seeking my advice and assistance in caring for them. I can still vividly remember one night when all of us girls had to call an ambulance for Jackie. She was laid out on the bathroom floor sweating profusely. Too weak to even speak. I thought she was surely going to die. She had suffered an allergic reaction after taking some penicillin in the medicine cabinet. The antibiotic had been prescribed to Dorothy for the strep throat she had been diagnosed with four months prior. Jackie had a sore throat and took it upon herself to use the medication. By the time Billie came home three days later, Jackie had been treated, observed and sent home. I had lied when the hospital administrators asked me where my parents were. "They're out of town on business," I had said, wishing it were true.

I reached the foyer and was instantly greeted by an acrid smell. It smelled like something was on fire. "What the heck," I said aloud. It was coming from upstairs. I hope I didn't leave my curling iron on or leave some incense burning near my spritz or something. I rushed up the stairs and searched my bedroom and the master bathroom. Nothing. The smell was everywhere and now it smelled like one of Leron's poopy diapers was burning. I had never encountered such a scent before. Before I could get to the nursery, I was distracted. I heard laughter coming from the attic. I knocked on the door twice. No answer, even the laughs ceased. "Jackie, do you know what that horrible smell is," I asked. Still, no answer. "Jackie, I'm coming up."

"No, I've got company," she finally shouted, "Um, and anyway, I don't know what you're talking about." I heard her snap at the anonymous acquaintances, "Be quiet." Then she turned her stereo on. I turned to walk away from the door, but it was obvious to me now that the pungent odor was coming from Jackie's quarters. I cracked the door, as I contemplated whether or not I was going to crash my sister's little party. "I told you we should've just done this at my old hang out," I heard a strange voice whisper just before Jackie turned her stereo on. O.k., I may regret this, but I'm going up, I thought. I ran up the stairs, all the while the smell getting stronger and when I reached the top, I wished I had stayed at work. If only I could be like the little girl in Oz-click my heels three times and be somewhere else. The glass object sitting in the middle of the table looked like a cross between a light bulb and a crazy straw. A short young man sitting comfortably on the hardwood floor, screamed an obscenity as he jumped, noticing me standing at the top of the stairs. The others hadn't heard the creaking stairs because Jackie's stereo was now turned up full blast. After the man screamed, the two women, who were sitting around the pipe as if they were worshipping at a temple, got up and grabbed their jackets and snatching the pipe, they all left the room like school kids, in a single file line. I could smell the horrible putrid scent embedded in their clothes as they walked by me. Yet the odor lingered.

I didn't say a word, I was giving my sister the opportunity to explain why she and the others had decided to transform my attic into a crack house. Even though I knew no explanation would suffice. Jackie had always done things which turned my stomach, but I never anticipated this. I was extremely disappointed, to say the least. My horror turned into disbelief as Jackie reprimanded me for entering her room uninvited. She couldn't be serious. She's smoking crack in my house and I'm the villain?

"Your brain must be fried," I shouted, interrupting her speech about the right to privacy, "In case you have forgotten, this is my house. I can go anywhere I please, anytime I please."

"I didn't plan for this to happen," Jackie said humbly, "It's not like I'm some fiend or something. This is only my second time trying it…Anyway, everybody whose somebody is doing it."

"Who told you that? That Daryl guy?" I continued, not giving her a chance to answer, "How could you do this. Even if you don't respect me, you could at least respect the fact that there are children here. If you're going to start bringing crackheads in my home, you've got to think about the danger you're putting me, your mother and those kids in."

"Oh, stop overreacting," Jackie shouted defensively, "You're always overreacting. I know those people. They're not thinking about doing anything to you or your precious home. They're not crackheads, they're just trying to have a little fun. If you'd get that stick from up your butt, maybe you'd have fun sometime too…I'm so tired of you telling everyone how to run their life. It's not like you're doing that great a job running your own. You've always thought you were better than the rest of us-telling us what to do. Just because Billie was married to your father don't mean nothing. As far as I'm concerned, you're still a bastard."

Before I could get a word in edgewise, Jackie continued,

"You ain't no better than the rest of us. Keep your little house, your little job and your little car. You still don't have nothing, that's why you stick your fat, ugly nose where it doesn't belong. When it's all said and done. You're still nothing."

And with those words, my sister, who had been packing as she rambled on, began walking down the stairs. "I'll be back a little later for the rest of my stuff."

There I stood, outraged and infuriated, the rancid stench of crack cocaine billowing over my head. She had taken my money and now my dignity…leaving before I had the chance to throw her out.

CHAPTER 18

NOT A ONE TIME THING

Billie had the nerve to question me as to why Jackie departed two weeks ago…as if I had mistreated her in some way. She took my sister's side even after I told her what Jackie had done. "You've gotta remember Jackie's having a rough time now. You should try to be understanding," she had urged.

I should be understanding? Despite loathing her, I allowed her to stay in my house. She brings junkies and an illegal substance in with her, and I should understand? To make matters worse, Gina had called me early this morning, crying. Even though I had planned to sleep in late, I sat straight up in bed. She needed me. She began by telling me she had gone to a party at one of her friend's apartment the previous night. Party, I thought. Well, isn't that nice, eight months pregnant and she's getting her groove on while Billie and I are stuck at home playing Go Fish with her kids.

"The party was that bad," I asked, referring to the fact that she was weeping.

"No," she replied, "It's what happened at the party."

Gina said she had decided to leave early after the party started getting out of hand. A rowdy crowd had showed up and a fight had taken place. The crowd had more than dancing and drinking on its mind. Drugs were everywhere. Just as Gina had talked two of her girlfriends into leaving with her, she spotted Jackie sitting in a corner of the living room. She was about to approach her when she noticed that Jackie was waiting her turn to sniff a line. "Coke?" I asked, sitting up once again in the bed, making sure I understood what she was alluding to. I had hoped the incident in the attic was one of her first and last encounters with drugs, but it hadn't been a one time thing.

"Yeah," Gina sobbed, "She was there with that Daryl ...I told you he was bad news, but you laughed at me. Now, there ain't no telling what's going to happen to her."

"What," I said, not expecting Gina to repeat herself. She was blaming me for Jackie's poor choice in men? I was just as saddened as she was that Jackie had decided to add another despicable chapter to the trashy novel she called life. We all had our problems, sure, but none of us would go near drugs. We had seen what it could do firsthand as we watched Edna deteriorate. Each of us had vowed that we'd never touch the stuff. Despite all my sisters had done, I don't think any of them had even tried pot before. Now, Jackie had chosen to run before she even crawled, jumping right into the heavy stuff first. Could it be my fault? Grandpa George used to always say a house is not destroyed without a warning. Had I ignored the warning? I doubt that Jackie would've listened to anything I had to say, but I could've tried.

"Angie....Angie," Gina called out over the receiver. I had forgotten she was on the phone.

"Yeah, I'm here."

"I'm sorry. I'm not trying to say it's your fault or anything. I'm just feeling real scared right about now. That's all."

"There's nothing else you could've done. You tried to talk to her," I reminded Gina, "She didn't listen. We've all got to make our own mistakes."

"Yeah, that's true. I guess I just needed to talk to someone about it," Gina responded, "I feel much better now."

I don't, I thought, as the conversation ended and I hung up the phone. I was feeling quite guilty. There had to be something I could do, but what?

"Thank you," I said to the woman behind the desk as she handed me a receipt and the key to the safe deposit box I had just purchased. Here I was again, in a place so familiar to me—sticking my nose where it didn't belong. I had gone into Jackie's room and rummaged through the remaining things. There was a lot of jewelry she hadn't pawned yet and there was some crystal and other expensive items. I grabbed everything of value I could find and brought it here where I placed it in a safe place. I can't explain what I was thinking. Maybe, I figured, Jackie would stop using if she didn't have anything else to sell. She'd realize how dangerous her behavior had been these past weeks or months. Only she knew for sure. "I'm helping," I said, trying to convince myself. Let it never be said that Angela didn't do her part to protect her family…never.

CHAPTER 19

NOBODY KNOWS THE TROUBLE I'VE SEEN

"What," I said, trying to understand what Billie was telling me, "Calm down. I don't know what you're saying."

I ran into Belinda as I was rushing toward the elevator. I had just informed my boss that I had a family emergency and was leaving for the day. I didn't greet my friend with the typical smile. I was too frightened to pretend that I was alright.

"Can't talk now. My sister's been rushed to the hospital," I whispered.

"I'll be praying for you," I heard Belinda say as the elevator doors closed.

All of the kids were home today so Billie said she had gone into Brandy's room to see if she'd take her and the children to the mall. Brandy appeared to be sleeping but Billie became hysterical when she couldn't wake her up and realized something was wrong. If one of the kids had not dialed 911, Brandy would still be lying motionless in her bed instead of being on her way to St. Barnabas Hospital. Billie said she smelled like she had taken a bath in whiskey…and my mother should know. After all, she had her share of alcohol rubs, pun intended.

I'm surprised I wasn't stopped on the way here. I broke every speed limit on my route. I just didn't want to risk getting to the hospital and being met by the words, "You're too late." The doctor said Brandy was a victim of alcohol poisoning. She had nearly drank herself into a coma. For the first time ever, I cried openly in front of my mother. Billie, who was also crying... silently, did not reach out to embrace me. Even though we were both going through a storm, she sought isolation as shelter. She walked over to the waiting room and plopped down in a seat. Laquesha, Leron, Wadell and Jaquan were all over me.

"What's going on Auntie?" they asked, almost in unison.

"Is Aunt Brandy going to be o.k.," Wadell questioned as one of the others shouted, "Is she dead" apathetically.

This was no place for children. I decided to take them home. Brandy was my sister and I wanted nothing more than to stay, but she was Billie's daughter.

"Billie, here's some money in case you want something to eat and here's my cell phone," I said, showing her how to use it, "Call me and let me know what's going on. After I get in touch with Gina, I'll be back."

She shook her head. "Are you going to be alright here by yourself," I asked, before finally leaving. She shook her head again.

I finally got in touch with Gina around four o'clock. For somebody with no job, she is unusually busy. I went to drop the kids off at her apartment, but she was waiting for me at the curb. "There's no food at my place," she explained. So, I had to drive all the way back to my house so she could stay there. "It's a shame, you have to ask somebody to babysit their own kids," I mumbled as I pulled out of the driveway.

I entered the waiting room and looked around for Billie. I hope everything's alright, I thought, as I realized she wasn't in there. She had only called me once to tell me that Brandy was in the Intensive Care Unit. She had started to come around before she vomited and choked on some of it. Now she was suffering from aspiratory pneumonia. I sat down and pretended to read a magazine even though my mind was far from skin care and celebrity interviews. Billie sat down beside me. "I went to get a soda," she explained, showing me the can of cola. Before I could respond, I noticed a familiar face. Belinda was waving in the doorway and she was accompanied by four strangers. I had called her at work just to further explain why I had hurried out of the work place. I didn't, however, tell her my sister had drank her way here. I never expected her to come, but here she was. I recognized one of the women with her as the preacher who had spoken the first night I had visited Belinda's church. One of the other women was the lady who had so eloquently informed me that more men were finding salvation.

"Who all those people," Billie snarled as she stared at the uninvited visitors.

"That is one of my friends from work and people from her church," I said as I waved and motioned for them to approach.

"Oh no, that's just what we need. Sanctimonious church folks knowing all our business. Who asked them to come? Don't they have a service to go to or something?" Billie snapped, looking at me as if I had breached a matter of national security.

She got up and walked out of the room.

"Was that your mother," Belinda asked, taking the seat Billie had occupied.

The other women sat next to her.

"Yep, that's her," I said, hoping she wouldn't return until Belinda and her friends left.

"We're all praying for you and your family," said the woman who had sat next to me at the revival.

Four weeks ago, I had sat beside her, an annoyed stranger. Now here I was, sitting in almost the exact position as before, touched by her kindness.

"Angela, this is Sister Michelle," Belinda said, giving the woman a name, "And this is Sister Rhonda, Sister Yasmin and Elder Smith."

"Hi, God bless you," each woman said, smiling as they were introduced.

"Nice to meet you," I said in return, "I didn't expect to see you."

"Well, I know this is a time when you and your family may want to be left alone, but we wanted to come down just in case Brandy had come out of the ICU. We were hoping we could pray for her, if that was o.k. with you."

"Oh, sure," I said, "As soon as she comes around." I didn't necessarily believe as they did, but I was willing to try anything to ensure my sister's recovery.

The women sat around with me for about forty-five minutes. We were talking and laughing. They really lifted my spirits. I felt a little awkward when I saw them with Belinda, but they proved to be a great source of comfort-sharing stories about tough situations they said the Lord had brought them through.

"He brought me through it, not around it," Michelle had remarked as she spoke candidly about her husband's heart attack, "God is so good. Some people think that if you have the Lord in your life, you don't have to go through anything anymore. That's not true. You still face problems but God helps you-not always by taking the problem away, but sometimes by giving you the strength to get through it. He's so so good."

As we sat, pondering on Michelle's words, Belinda interrupted the silence, suggesting they leave so I could be alone with my mother. I have to admit, I was a little sad to see them walking away. The women had hugged me and were approaching the door, all except Elder Smith. She had been relatively quiet, until now. She sat down next to me and looked directly in my eyes.

"Baby, I know you don't know me," she began, "But the entire time that I've been here, the Lord's been speaking to my spirit about you. I know that you have been trying to be in control of every aspect of your life... all your life. The Lord said it's time you let him take over. I know you feel like everything's out of control lately, but that's just because you're trying to be God...trying to be everything to everybody. I know you don't believe like I do right now. Maybe, you feel like God's let you down in the past so you're afraid to trust him. We will never understand everything. Some things we won't ever get answers to. My advice to you-let go and let God."

The diminutive woman, who appeared to be in her late 50's, handed me a small red bible which contained Psalms and the New Testament.

"Read St. Luke," she said, "The passage is already marked."

And with that said, she kissed me on the forehead the way a mother does her sleeping child and she walked away. This is too weird, I thought. She's done it again. She's read my whole life like it was a book. Now I know what Roberta Flack meant when she sang, "...telling my life with his words, killing me softly with his song, killing me softly with his song." Elder Smith hadn't sang a song, but she couldn't have paraphrased my pain any better if she had. I know Belinda couldn't have told her all that because she doesn't really know anything about me. Furthermore, I hadn't said anything during the conversation today that would lead anyone to believe my life was anything but normal. I had even breathed a breath of fresh air when the women didn't ask me what landed Brandy in the hospital. Belinda had told them she was found unconscious and that was that. After all, that's all I had told her. Now, here this woman was once again intruding -knowing things she had no right to know. Nevertheless, I accepted the bible.

Billie came back soon after they left. "Good, they're gone," she said, frowning, "Don't let those people fill your head with crap Angela. They're not concerned about you. They just want to know your business." Billie always had a way of raining on my parade. To think, for a moment I was at peace, thinking that maybe somebody cared. Not this time, I thought, she would not turn this thing around. They hadn't even asked me anything, they had just been there. Something Billie knew absolutely nothing about. "Everybody doesn't have alterior motives," I responded, turning my thoughts back to Brandy.

CHAPTER 20

DENIAL IS NOT A RIVER IN EGYPT

"What's up with her," I asked.

"What do you mean," Belinda said.

"She doesn't know me, but yet she knows a lot about me," I clarified.

Belinda chuckled and informed me that Elder Smith was a woman of God, a prophetess. She has a close relationship with God and wants to help others get one too, according to Belinda. I started not to ask her about the preacher, but I had to know more about her. She sure knew enough about me. I decided there was no time like the present when Belinda called my house to check on my sister.

The doctor said Brandy was improving daily. She had been moved out of ICU and was considered to be in stable condition. The toxins were out of her system and the fluid was no longer in her lungs, but they had urged her to stay a couple more days so the doctors could observe her before sending her home. They had also suggested that Brandy talk to a psychologist on staff before being discharged from the hospital. In the ICU, only her family had been allowed to visit, but now she could have other visitors as well. Belinda and her entourage had been to the hospital a few times during the week, each time praying for her and holding her hand. Brandy had been very receptive to all of them. She liked them and it showed.

Billie, on the other hand, would always leave when they came.

"Why do they keep coming back? Brandy doesn't even know them. Keep your holy roller friends away from her. She's been through enough," she protested, as if people praying could injure her further. Billie had even asked me if I was paying them to come visit Brandy. She must've seen a lot of horrible things in her life, I thought. Elder Smith had not returned and I was relieved. I didn't want to have to tell her that I still had not read the passage she highlighted for me.

Gina had been complaining about being left at home with the kids. "I want to see Brandy," she moaned, "She's my sister too." Every time we returned from a visit, she'd go on and on about how Wadell had spilled juice or how Leron didn't listen...blah, blah, blah. What did she think children did, sit still with their hands in their lap? I knew more about parenting than she did. Billie stayed home one evening with the children so Gina could visit Brandy. On the way home from the hospital, I told Gina she'd have to watch the kids again. "We promised Brandy we'd bring her some fish," I explained. Gina picked up right where she left off.

"I don't know Angie, I'm tired. They don't really listen to me...and I don't know what to do when I'm with them for a long time. I need a break. Remember, I am pregnant. Maybe, Billie could go to the hospital alone and you watch the kids."

"And how is Billie supposed to get there if I'm home," I responded.

"Maybe Dorothy can take her," Gina suggested.

"C'mon, you know she's on lock down half the time."

It was true. Dorothy was committed to several organizations. She spent a lot of her time doing volunteer work since she had been forbidden to even look for a full-time job. Dorothy spent hours in soup kitchens, homeless shelters and she was like a big sister to over a dozen girls at some youth center. She'd rush home and make dinner so it would be ready when Glen got home. He didn't know about all of her service. He liked her to stay home during the day. Sometimes when he called home and couldn't reach her, she'd lie and say she had been sleeping. My sister wasn't allowed to go out in the evening without Glen, not because he feared for her safety, but because he was afraid she might be meeting up with some guy. So if she wanted to go somewhere once he got home, she couldn't, unless he was willing to go with her. Needless to say, he had not been willing to come to the hospital. I think he was scared to face Billie and I. We had made our opinions of him quite clear in the past- one of the few times my mother and I agreed regarding a man's character. Dorothy had visited Brandy a few times during the day and after putting her foot down, she was permitted to visit one evening... without her boyfriend. She came to the hospital with a bruise on her cheek, more than likely, a punishment for her defiance. She couldn't really enjoy her visit because Glen kept beeping her and she spent more time on the phone than she did with Brandy.

"I'm sorry Gina," I continued, "I'm going to the hospital tomorrow. I already promised."

The matter was settled. Gina would have to watch her kids. Since she had been granting me this favor, I had suggested that she stay with me the entire week-to make things easier for her. It wouldn't kill her to stay in my house one more night.

The next day, I came home from work to change my clothes and pick Billie up so we could head to the hospital. As soon as I pulled up, I knew the night wasn't going to go smoothly. Jackie's BMW was parked in the driveway. Since she left, she had called and spoken to Billie a couple times, but she and I had not spoken since the crack incident and I was not looking forward to ending the silence. She hadn't even visited Brandy and I know Billie told her she was in the hospital.

"Oh, boy," I sighed, as I sat behind the steering wheel imagining what might take place upon me entering the house. I sighed again before turning the car off and pulling my key out of the ignition. I walked to the door like a man on death row walks to the electric chair. I grabbed the mail and headed straight toward the kitchen. I heard Jackie's voice before I even reached the doorway. She turned toward me and if looks could kill, I would've surely dropped dead.

"Where is my stuff Angie," she asked immediately.

"Oh, what a surprise. No hello, how ya doing or anything," I remarked sarcastically.

"Look, I don't have time to play games with you. I went upstairs to get some more of my things. Everything's out of place and some of my stuff is gone. Where is it?"

Jackie didn't appear to be the addict Gina had made her out to be. Her hair was stacked neatly in a bun on top of her head and she was wearing a black cat suit with an oversized gold loop belt, hung just below her waist. I had realized a long time ago that taking her stuff was silly. I would've given her the safe deposit box key and told her to get her stuff, but now it was a matter of principle. She had violated my home and she still had not even apologized.

"I don't know what you're talking about," I said, wishing I didn't.

"I'm gonna ask you one more time. Where are my things..."

"Good, then I only have to answer you once more. I don't have your stuff..."

Before I could finish my sentence, Jackie had jumped on me, knocking me to the floor. My reflexes hadn't even had time to react when I felt the blow to my head and the warmth of my own blood trickle down my face. The little tramp had punched me in the nose. I've never been one to back out of a fight so I grabbed Jackie's arms as hard as I could, giving no consideration to the bleeding or the almost unbearable pains shooting across the bridge of my nose. We rolled back and forth on the linoleum until I finally pinned her down. Billie had been screaming something the entire time, but I had tuned her out. Now here she was, pulling me off of my sister and yelling at me as if I had started the brawl. Like I had left my job thinking, boy, I can't wait to get home and kick some butt. Gina and her kids were standing at the top of the basement stairs. I had to tell her ignorant behind that this was no scene for children to witness. "Take them back downstairs," I yelled. Gina did as I commanded. I grabbed the dish towel on the counter and put it to my face, hoping it would stop the bleeding. Jackie looked as if she might lunge at me again so I picked up the phone and told her I was going to call the police unless she left at that moment. "This isn't over yet," she shouted as Billie dragged her to the door, patting her wounds-a few scratches-with a wet cloth.

The dish towel was soaked by this time and blood began to drip onto the floor. I ran to the bathroom to get a glimpse of the damage in the mirror. I suspected immediately what the emergency room doctor later confirmed, my nose was broken. When I got home that night, Billie was waiting for me.

"I don't know why you couldn't have just given her things to her Angela. All this would've never happened. She has a right to her stuff...and you both nearly sent Gina into labor with all that commotion."

I didn't open my mouth. There were no words in the English language that could describe my pain. The doctor had given me Ibuprofen to alleviate the pain in my nose, but no prescription could ease the pain in my heart.

"I don't know why you girls do what you do," Billie continued, "I did my best. I tried to make up for your fathers, who didn't care nothing about ya'll. I was always there, but I guess that wasn't good enough. One of you having babies left and right, the other trying to kill herself, Dorothy letting some man take advantage of her and now, you and Jackie rolling around beating each other senseless. It just don't make no sense."

Billie's tirade persisted for at least ten more minutes, but I left the room before it concluded. She had never once even stopped to ask me if I was alright. I guess she just assumed the gauze on my nose, which seemed bigger than my head, was nothing more than a sophisticated bandage. I don't know why Billie never cared for me. After all, I loved her with every part of my being. She was my mother. My heart was pounding and disappointment seemed to linger in my veins. I felt as though I was going to explode, but no tears had fallen. I walked up the stairs, leaning on the banister as if it were a crutch. Once I reached my bedroom, I closed the door. My legs grew weak and I could barely stand. I fell to my knees and the floor received them with a loud thud! As my legs buckled, the tears fell. I was trying to catch my breath, but I was drowning in my own tears. I didn't have the strength to wipe them. With my heart racing, my palms sweating and my mind spinning, I gasped, "Help."

CHAPTER 21

A LIVING TESTIMONY

Brandy had talked to the psychologist, and the doctors, after reading his recommendation, were discharging her. "Tomorrow, she's free to go," Dr. Spivak had said. Even though she was physically fine, I knew her recovery was yet to be complete. However, I had already been attacked by one sister, I had no intention of provoking another by butting in.

I was glad to see Belinda enter the room, holding a balloon and a card. Brandy was also happy to see her. You couldn't tell by looking at them that they had just met seven days prior. They seemed like old friends. The three of us chatted for over an hour like we were at a sleepover. The conversation shifted, however, after Belinda began talking about life choices.

"I have been talking to Brandy about the things that led to her hospitalization," she said matter-of-factly.

I could feel my eyes widen with surprise. I was so embarrassed, I wanted to vanish. At the same time, I was curious as to why Brandy had chosen to share such a personal story with someone she barely knew. She had never even opened up to family, but now she found it so easy to spill her guts to Belinda.

"I told Brandy that I understood her pain," Belinda said, appearing to read my mind, "I am a recovering alcoholic."

Belinda, an alcoholic? She had to be joking. She had everything together. In fact, in a lot of ways, I saw her as the complete opposite of me. Now she was expecting me to believe she used to have a drinking problem. I had seen alcoholism up close and she did not fit the profile.

"After my mom died, I became extremely depressed," Belinda expounded, "We were very close. She was a preacher and I had been raised in the church. So, when she passed away and I felt myself getting angry with God, I panicked. I figured I couldn't be saved and feel what I felt so all hope was lost. I started drinking to cover up my pain, but then I kept drinking to forget my guilt. I became so helpless and so hopeless that soon I didn't care if I lived or died. I would've been lost forever if my cousin hadn't ministered to me. And even when it seemed like I wasn't listening, she was praying for me. See, everything was alright when I was a closet alcoholic-I could still do my job, I could still take care of my responsibilities. The problem is that every closet drinker has got to come out in the open one day. It gets pretty stuffy in there. What you do in the dark will always come out in the light. The moment of truth came for me one night when I decided to get behind the wheel of my car after having a few drinks. I wasn't staggering and I didn't reek of alcohol, but I still shouldn't have driven. To make a long story short, I ran off the side of a road. Miraculously I, like my car, only sustained a few scratches, but it made me stop and think, 'what am I doing here? Would my mother be proud of who I had become? I need help'. I knew the next time I wouldn't be so blessed. I realized by drinking I was hurting myself and I had the potential to harm others. Sitting there on the side of that road, with my warning lights flashing-I asked God to hear my cry, to deliver me. I told God I no longer wanted to be the way I was. Whoever says prayer doesn't change things, never prayed before. When my plea had ended, I turned the flashing lights off and drove home. I felt a peace I had never known until then. I knew as long as I did what I was supposed to, God would do what I asked…and here I am, ten years later, sober, happily married with two children and having a daily love affair with the Lord.

Brandy sat in her hospital bed absorbing every word that left Belinda's mouth like a sponge. I couldn't help, but be a little envious. All the years I've given Brandy advice, I've never seen her as attentive and enlightened as she was now. Belinda offered to pray with Brandy as she had prayed for herself a decade ago. Brandy was a little reluctant, but she agreed and Belinda grabbed her hand. As she reached for mine, I informed her I had to leave.

"I'm late for an appointment," I said abruptly.

I hugged them both and exited. I got outside the room, and I could hear my co-worker's voice as she called on a redeemer I had never known and doubted I ever would.

I had nowhere to go, so I ended up at the last place I wanted to be-home. As soon as I entered the door, I heard the phone ringing. It was obvious that no one was planning to answer it, so I ran to pick it up as if it were someone calling to speak to me.

"Hello, may I speak to Jackie Roberts," the voice on the other end said.

"Jackie isn't here right now. May I take a message?"

"Can you please inform her that she still has not paid the balance she owes on her rental unit at Kravitz and Son Storage. She's emptied it so I assume she no longer plans to utilize it. However, she must've forgotten to pay the remaining fee," he said.

"There must be some mistake. It can't be completely empty," I interrupted.

"Oh, I'm certain it is. She left the keys at the front desk, but she didn't pay the balance. I'm sure it just slipped her mind," the caller continued, "My name is Raymond Parker and I can be reached at..."

I allowed the man to finish before hanging up the phone. I wanted to believe that Jackie had moved her furniture, along with Brandy's, to a different storage facility. I wanted to believe that Mr. Parker's assumption was correct, that it had slipped her mind to pay off the money she owed, but my good sense prevented that. How could Billie defend this, I wondered. I decided not to give her the satisfaction of trying. I also decided that it would be a while before I told Brandy that her sister had stolen her furniture. As long as she stayed with me, she wouldn't need it anyway.

CHAPTER 22

CONFESSION

The wind whistled softly as the yellow and orange leaves danced. The scene was peaceful. Most people were probably turning the thermostat up in their homes and spending their Sunday afternoon cozied up in front of the television. Here I was, sitting on the patio like it was a summer day. After putting on my jacket, I had pulled one of the white plastic patio chairs out of the basement and brought it outside shamelessly. The kids were inside fighting and Billie had the radio blasting like she was at some club. Dorothy had gotten permission to visit us for a few hours today. She wanted to cook a traditional Sunday meal. She said it was awful that we ate out so much on Sundays. So she was bustling around the kitchen preparing smothered chicken, cabbage, mashed potatoes with gravy and homemade biscuits. She had to make enough to take home because Glen was accustomed to having a home cooked meal every day. The house quickly filled with the heavenly aroma only soul food can bring. While no one was looking I decided to steal a moment of peace. Despite the chill in the air, the weather was beautiful. I looked around at the manicured lawn proudly. I never let the grass get unsightly. I had always cut the lawn, trimmed the bushes and in the winter I shoveled, almost the minute snow particles left the clouds. I found myself daydreaming when suddenly I heard the patio door slide open. Brandy was standing in the door, wearing a smile and her Sunday best. She had just come home from church.

She squatted down and sat on the three steps that led to the patio.

"What you doing out here," she asked, pulling her black quarter-length coat closed.

"Just enjoying the weather…How was church?" I asked, pretending to care.

"Good," Brandy replied, "Pastor Ellis talked about the Prodigal Son, how he went away from his father and got all wild. Then when his friends were gone along with his money, he…"

"I know the story," I said, interrupting.

After all, I had spent a lot of my childhood in the church. Since Brandy had begun visiting Belinda's church, you would've thought I needed one of those books-Church for Dummies. She was always expounding on some scripture. I guess she was just excited.

"Snippy, snippy," Brandy said, still smiling. After a long pause, she began to speak again, "You know Angie, I've technically been an alcoholic since I was about eleven…You know how Billie used to blame Edna for watering down her stash? Well, it wasn't Edna, it was me."

Where did that come from, I thought. I didn't know why she had chosen to open up to me now, but I was honored she trusted me enough to do so.

Brandy continued, "I was so glad when I became a teenager because then Billie would let me go out clubbing with her, and I could drink openly. But even then, I was careful not to drink too much. I didn't want her to get suspicious. I was never worried that she'd beat me for drinking a lot, I just didn't want her to find out I'd been drinking up her stuff. I knew I'd get a butt whooping for sure if she found that out."

Another pause. I didn't know whether to comment or just keep listening. My sister made the decision for me because she kept talking.

"The first time I snuck some, I felt so powerful. I felt in control. I had gotten away with it. The next time, I discovered I kinda liked the taste of it and before long, I was drinking enough to give me a little buzz. For a few hours I could forget about the mice living in my closet or the hunger pangs in my stomach. I could pretend that the men who came by to see Billie were just friends and that those who made me feel dirty when they hugged me, actually were my "uncles", as Billie made me call them. After a while I needed to drink. As I got older, I no longer found it a thrill to risk a beating, so I got a job so I could buy my own liquor. I stayed in control though, or so I thought…until Sharif. You know, that last boyfriend I had. I really loved him, but not enough to stay sober. He left and I just found myself not caring anymore so I started drinking at lunchtime—anytime. I can't tell you how much of my life has been wasted 'cause of this."

I had no idea how I should reply. I felt stupid for being so envious of Belinda and Brandy's relationship. She was helping my sister gain control of her life. I should've been grateful.

"You've been carrying me Angie and I just want to thank you… and I thought I owed you some kind of explanation, that's all," said Brandy as she brushed her coat off and headed back indoors.

If she only knew what I had been thinking these past few weeks, she'd know I didn't deserve her gratitude. As I watched her chatting with Dorothy, I couldn't help but feel proud-not of me, but of her. She's going to be alright, I said to myself.

CHAPTER 23

NO ROOM AT THE INN

I was so happy Gina was taking some kind of stand. With her due date a couple weeks away, all anyone could talk about was the arrival of the new baby. Billie kept saying she didn't think Gina was going to be able to take care of another baby, as if she was taking care of the ones she already had. I had understood when Gina left Wadell and Laquesha here. She could barely take care of herself, let alone two children. It was supposed to be a temporary arrangement-just until she got herself together. But then, when Jaquan was about a year old, Billie told Gina he could stay too. "Angela knows you not on your feet yet," she had said. It seems like Leron has lived here almost since birth. No one had notified me about his change of address either. Billie kept him for a weekend and he never went home. So you can imagine how ecstatic I was when Gina told Billie she was keeping this baby with her. Instead of encouraging her, Billie kept reminding her of her limitations.

"You don't have no car, no job, no man. How you goin' do that by yourself-especially living on the other side of town? You just goin' end up bringing that baby here all the time anyway."

When all of the negative talk failed, Billie came up with another plan. "Why don't you just move in the attic? Jackie's gone and the way her and Angela been going at it, I doubt she's ever coming back." Now, granted my house is a nice size, but Billie must've thought she was a cast member of Dynasty and we were living on an estate. I sat completely dumbstruck, awaiting Gina's response. I nearly did a cartwheel when she stood her ground.

"I'm going to try it on my own for a while Billie and if that doesn't work, I'll take you up on your offer."

Her offer? But it wasn't *her* house. I had bought Gina a bassinet when Wadell was born. I never got a chance to discard it or give it away since she had need of it just about every year. So, I pulled it out of the storage section of the basement, pulled off the plastic I had wrapped it in and dusted it off to make sure it was in the best condition possible. There really was no need to go to Baby Palace or hold a shower since I had kept everything from walkers to high-chairs. I even had a carseat in the garage. But because I was so elated that the bundle of joy would not be cuddling up at my house, I bought Gina a crib and a changing table. The crib I had purchased for her before was upstairs in the room Leron and Jaquan shared.

I knew Gina needed bottles, pacifiers and such, so I also decided to throw her a shower, hoping it would be her last. All of her "ghetto-fabulous" friends came with designer outfits, appropri-ate for either gender, wrapped underneath their arms. They came sporting green hair, red hair, purple hair, blue eyes they hadn't been born with and sneakers that cost more than some of my suits. I felt like I was hosting a Halloween party. Some had caught the bus to show their support, while I played taxi for the others-transporting them and their gifts. Gina was so happy-so I guess it had been worth the hassle. At least that's what I thought until Gina's water broke. Her best friend Tora drove her and Billie to the hospital and I was left with the Dr. Seuss rejects. I didn't feel like driving all the way across town to drop off the people it seemed like I had just picked up, so I decided the bash must go on. I was left listening to gangsta rap and stories about people's babies' daddies.

Tonya Marie Roberts was born five hours later. Gina had named her after her father whom she hadn't seen since she was four months pregnant. Go figure!

I had dreamed of having a daughter one day. Then, I could be the kind of mother to her that I always wished Billie had been to me. I would shower her with affection, encourage her to be anything she dreamed of becoming…and put diamond earrings in her ear. Well, quickly approaching thirty, I began to have doubts that I'd ever get married or have a child. So, when my niece was still a baby, I bought her some small diamond earrings and got her ears pierced. I came to the hospital holding a velvet jewelry box. I had bought Tonya some earrings similar to her sister's. No matter what the circumstances surrounding her conception were, I wanted her to know she was a gem. Something I had longed to hear all of my life.

CHAPTER 24

EXODUS

I had never seen someone be so excited and so frightened at the same time. Dorothy was thrilled that she had finally enrolled in the GED course, but she couldn't help looking over her shoulder every time she left the house-fearing Glen would find out about her whereabouts. Her fear inevitably became reality when her instructor called her apartment one night, and she had to face his wrath. I was not surprised to see Dorothy on my doorstep. Nana called and told me she had left. "I think it may be for good this time," she said, "At least I hope it is. She deserves better. She's a special lady, ain't that right?" I hadn't shared Nana's foresight at first. I had watched Dorothy be degraded for years. She had suffered everything from bloody noses to broken arms. Nothing had been enough to make her leave. Battered and bruised, she came to me, but this time she had come with a different perspective. "I'm not going back," she sobbed, obviously torn apart by her decision.

I was elated. I had urged Dorothy to leave many times, but all of my pleas seemed to fall on deaf ears...until now. I wish I could take the credit for her courageous move, but I learned that someone much smaller than me had inspired her exodus. "I'm pregnant," Dorothy announced two weeks after moving into my house. I hadn't even bothered to ask her why she had decided to leave the love of her life, for fear that my questions would stir up too many emotions and she'd end up back in her abuser's arms.

"I love this baby. This child makes me want to be a better person. That's why I'm going to go back to school...I just can't live the way I've been living. I refuse to bring a child into that," she said.

It amazed me how much she had matured and how quickly. I guess carrying a child can do that. Dorothy had only been in the house a few days when the phone calls began. "Tramp, slut, ho," and any other derogatory name Glen could think of echoed over the phone lines. When the terrifying approach didn't work, then he'd call crying like a baby, telling Dorothy how much he missed her and how he couldn't live without her. I changed my phone number and made sure it wasn't listed. I knew Glen didn't have the balls to come to my house, but I still persuaded Dorothy to file a temporary restraining order against him. Now, his cowardice was a matter of record.

Dorothy was confident that she was doing the right thing, but it was easy to see that she missed her batterer. Despite her longing to see him and tell him about the miracle they had created, she knew her life was worthwhile because of her sacrifice. She passed the GED with flying colors and is looking forward to enrolling in a community college.

She wasn't the only one making changes. Brandy joined a support group at a local hospital and she has become a regular at Greater Love. I had even visited more, at her urging. I have to admit, I never left disappointed. The message always seemed to be tailored just for me. My life seemed to be more balanced now. There was the bad, but now there was the good also. I could face my fears.

As I dabbed my cheeks with the astringent-soaked cotton ball, preparing myself for bed, I thought back to everything Elder Smith had told me. Throwing the cotton in the garbage, I walked over to the dresser where I kept the bible she had so graciously given me. Not knowing what I'd find, I sat on the edge of the bed and flipped to the page with the bookmark exposed. Luke 6:47-49 read:

> "Whoever comes to Me and hears my sayings and
> does them, I will show you whom he is like: he is like
> a man building a house, who dug deep and laid the

foundation on the rock and when the flood arose, the stream beat vehemently against that house and could not shake it, for it was founded on the rock. But he who heard and did nothing is like a man who built a house on the earth without a foundation, against which the stream beat vehemently and immediately it fell and the ruin of that house was great."

I read the scripture twice. The message was clear, but I didn't want to meditate on it right then. Instead, I tied the silk periwinkle scarf on my head and slipped beneath the flannel sheets, waiting for Dorothy to enter. Since her arrival, she had become more than a sister, she was more like a best friend. We spent every night sitting in the bed, laughing and watching television until we could no longer keep our eyes open. Life was good.

CHAPTER 25

THE TRUTH AND NOTHING BUT THE TRUTH

B oy, am I thirsty, I thought, as I gulped the iced tea. Aunt Lizzy
sat on the opposite side of the booth slurping down orange
soda. "So what's this about," I asked. I had been curious ever since
she called me and asked me to meet her for dinner. I had only seen
my aunt three times since my sixteenth birthday so I really didn't
understand why she took an interest in me now.

"I'm selling the house," she said solemnly, "We've been want-
ing to move to the south. Now Rich has a job opportunity in
Atlanta. We agree it's time."

"Oh, wow," I responded, completely ignorant as to why she had
chosen to share her relocation plans with me.

She could do whatever she wanted with the house. It was hers. I
never had a desire to step foot in the home since my grandparents
died. Its worth had diminished drastically as far as I was concerned.
Grandma Helen and Grandpa George had brought life to the prop-
erty, now it was just a mere lot.

"Well, I can't leave until I have finally given you what's yours,"
Aunt Lizzy said vaguely.

What's mine? I thought. I hadn't owned anything in that house
for almost fifteen years.

"Here," my aunt continued, as she slid a shoebox across the

table, "Mom had these in the attic. She never gave these to you 'cause she didn't want to bring you girls anymore pain. I didn't give them to you because I thought it would be cruel to do so when you were going to live with her."

"Her? Her, who?...Billie?" I asked, "What is this? You've got to tell me more than this."

My aunt gave no further explanation. She simply told me to open the box. She promised to put an end to all of my questions once I opened it. I did not know why, but my heart began to palpitate as I pulled the cardboard lid off of the box. It was filled with about a dozen letters-all addressed to Billie.

"Billie's mail?" I asked, pausing to take another sip of tea.

Aunt Lizzy looked pensive.

"I don't know how much you know about your mom and dad," she began, "I mean about their history. James met Billie while he was visiting some relatives in Alabama. Our family was acquainted with Josie, Billie's grandmother and Annie, Billie's mother. Josie was a very religious woman, but Annie sort of had a...a reputation. Everyone used to say she was messing with some white man. Josie, on the other hand, thought she could do no wrong. Annie was her little angel and she stuck by her, but eventually Annie got pregnant and after Billie was born, it was obvious to everyone that the rumor had been true. The church folks were really cruel, especially since the white man was married. Annie skipped town and left Josie to raise Billie. From what mom told me, Josie saw Billie as a constant reminder of her little girl's sin. There was no room in her heart for anyone, but Annie, so Billie spent her life trying to win her grandmother over. When she was still a teenager, she met your dad and they fell in love. Mom did not approve of them seeing each other and so they began to court secretly. He told mom that Billie was miserable in her grandmother's house and she wanted to come to Jersey with him. Mom hit the roof and she made James come home immediately, but not soon enough. Billie turned up pregnant and even though my mom always believed she trapped James, ultimately she believed in doing the right thing, so they got married. Mom insisted Billie and James live with her and dad for a while because they wanted him to finish school, but Billie and mom just couldn't get along. Your dad was in a constant tug of war, so after Billie kept begging, he moved out and they got their own place. He got a job and wouldn't let anyone help him. He wanted to prove he was a man..."

"What does all this have to do with the mail," I interrupted. I was interested in finding out about my parents, but I didn't understand how the shoebox and the story related.

"I'm getting to that," she replied, "Well, the pressure got to be too much and he left, as you know. My parents were extremely disappointed. What you don't know is, that a few months after he left, he called my parents and told them how ashamed he was for what he had done. He mentioned that he had written to Billie in hopes that they could reconcile. They didn't hear from him for a while and we all started to get worried. Mom and dad had tried to report him missing, but the police would not search for a grown man who had walked out on his family voluntarily. Dad was just about to hire a private investigator when James called them one night. I was over the house and I remember mom crying and begging him to come home. When they got off the phone, mom said he had threatened to kill himself. He said he couldn't live without..." Lizzy gulped, as a tear glided down her cheek, "Without his girls. He said Billie never wrote him back even though he had enclosed the address where he had been staying in recent weeks. When he hung up that night, mom was distraught. She made dad take her to Billie's apartment right then. They confronted her and she handed the letters over to them. They went to the motel where James had been, but he was no longer there."

"I don't understand. Why wouldn't Billie write him back?" I questioned.

"Well, no one's ever asked her," my aunt replied, "But by the time your father wrote, she had already changed quite a bit...drinking...men. She couldn't go back, she was already immersed into that lifestyle. Dad always said the rejection had been too much for her. After all, she had been rejected all her life."

"What happened to him," I asked, afraid to hear the response.

"No one really knows. Dad always feared that he had gone somewhere and followed through on his threat, but mom never wanted to believe that. She went and got you girls and she said when he called again, she would tell him that he didn't have to live without his girls because you were with her. Needless to say, he never called. Mom and dad even put his name in the will, hoping they'd find him one day. These are the letters he wrote to Billie. Mom wanted to give them to you girls. She wanted you to know how much your father loved you, but dad said that would just poison you against your mother... and it was James who just up and left. She reluctantly compromised, vowing to give them to you on your sixteenth birthday, but she wasn't around. I knew the whole story, but I wasn't going to be the one to cause animosity, especially when you and Rosa had to go live with her after mom and dad died."

"Why now?" I asked, bewildered, pushing back tears.

"I didn't want to throw them away, but I don't want to take them with me either. So, I figured, it was time."

"I can't believe this," I uttered. I would've said more, but I was speechless.

I didn't stick around for the appetizer I had ordered. I grabbed my "inheritance", said a quick unaffectionate goodbye to my aunt and got in my car. As I pulled into South Mountain Reservation, I wondered if I should go through with my plan. The old reservation was like a huge, serene park. It was a great place to think. Trees surrounded me like football players in a huddle and I could hear the faint sound of crickets in the background. I grabbed the first letter, holding it in my lap, I hesitated. I knew that if I read my father's words, my life would never be the same.

I read each letter several times. Even though they had just been thrown into the box, it wasn't difficult to figure out the order in which they had been written. Each was more intense than the last. The tone of the correspondence went from sad to distraught as my father begged for Billie's forgiveness and described his eagerness to return home. In one letter, he referred to coming to her apartment and the pain he felt because she wouldn't let him see his kids. What? Had he just been feet away from me, yet too far to grasp? The moon was full and the light from it shone into my windshield. Despite the glare, I had to turn the light on in the car so I could read the words which I had almost memorized.

If I had ever doubted before, I was certain now that my father loved us. All those years, feelings of rejection and abandonment had wrapped around my heart like a python wraps around its prey. Now, I discovered it didn't have to be that way. Billie had told me my father didn't love me. Her lie had haunted me. I was relieved, yet I was also furious. How could anyone be so evil that they'd palm their pain off on an innocent, unsuspecting child. My mind shifted immediately to Rosa, for she, too, had been a victim of Billie's deceit. I thought of calling her and exposing our mother for the liar she is, but what good would that do? Rosa already despised Billie. This would just make her hate her more, if that were possible. No, I wouldn't share this with her.

I slammed the door as I entered the house. I didn't care who I disturbed. I wanted the world to know I had been wronged. I could hear Wadell and Laquesha upstairs screaming at each other. Dorothy was in the middle of trying to be a mediator when I shut the door.

"Hey, Ang, that you," she shouted, simultaneously shushing our nephew and niece.

"Yeah," I yelled back, heading for the stairs.

Wait a minute, I said to myself. This hadn't been one of Billie's typical irresponsible actions. I couldn't just sweep this under the rug. I wouldn't!! It had been hidden for too long already. I couldn't run from this fight.

"Billie," I yelled-now making my way to the basement door, "Come up here, NOW!!"

"Angela, are you crazy-screaming through the house like a mad woman. I'm getting Leron ready for bed. I'll be up in a minute."

"NOW," I reiterated at the top of my voice.

Billie, taken aback by my rudeness, stomped up the stairs with Leron on her left hip and his pajama pants in her right hand. She was wearing a scowl and looked as though she was coming upstairs to spank me, but before she could remark, I said,

"I can't believe you did this," waving the shoebox in front of me, "I put up with a lot. I've forgiven you for screwing up my childhood. Even when I lived with Grandma and Grandpa, my life was far from perfect because I still had to face the fact that you were my mother. I forgave you for stealing my childhood-I spent it worrying about you and trying to figure out how to get you to stay sober for more than a week. I forgave you for putting my sisters in harm's way, time and time again, for embarrassing me by surrounding yourself with the scum of the universe. I forgave you for driving Rosa away-for stripping me of my closest friend. I forgave you for overlooking my success and taking me and everything I've done for you for granted...but I cannot, I will not ever forgive you for this. How dare you take it upon yourself to decide whether or not I needed my father in my life. I can understand if you couldn't forgive him for walking out, but how dare you never give us a chance to."

Pacing back and forth, I started to throw the box at her, but I didn't want to lose the only thing I had left of my father. So, I clutched the letters and continued, "I don't know how different my life might be today if you had, but I know it would be different..."

"You don't know what you're talking 'bout. You don't know the whole story. You don't know..."

Before Billie could finish, I screamed.

"I know that my life has been a living hell because of you. I know Brandy is an alcoholic because of you. I know Dorothy has been stitched up more than a quilt because of you. Jackie is a gold-digging, drug-feigning ho because of you Billie. Rosa is off acting like her parents are dead because that fantasy is better than this reality...and let's not even talk about Gina. I don't know much MOM, but I know that. You're always going on and on about how much of a mess your kids' lives are in-always running around asking, 'why, oh, why'. Well, look in the mirror. Oh, you are so right. I don't know everything, but I know enough. I know enough to say that I don't know where you're going to go, but you've got to get the heck out of here!"

By this time, the kitchen was crowded. Brandy was standing in the doorway along with Dorothy, Laquesha and Wadell. Even my nephew Jaquan had climbed up the basement steps to get a peak at the spectacle. Normally, I'd apologize to everyone for causing the commotion, but today I didn't care.

"What ya'll looking at," I asked, "This is my house and I'll make as much noise as I darn well please."

With those words, I made my way through my sisters in the

door and stormed up the stairs. I was sitting on the edge of the bed, waiting for the guilt to set in. How could I have spoken that way to my mother...and then to top it off, throw her into the street. I was waiting, but I still didn't feel remorseful. Actually, I felt relieved, refreshed, rejuvenated...reborn. I had never so much as raised my voice at my mother before. Even though she had done horrible things-so many, as a matter of fact, that I don't even think God, himself, would blame me for being angry-she was still my mother. The woman who brought me into the world. However, I had years of animosity bottled up inside me. I meant everything I had just said to her. I had wanted to say those things for a long time, but I just couldn't bring myself to do it, for fear that I would hurt Billie's feelings. I never wanted to hurt her-even now, but I could not excuse this last betrayal. Life had been one giant wrestling match and Billie had finally made me say, 'uncle'.

CHAPTER 26

TAKE THIS AND CALL ME IN THE MORNING

I must've fallen asleep because I found myself wiping slob from the corners of my mouth when I heard the knocks on my bedroom door. I opened the door and there stood my sisters. Oh, here we go, I thought, they're going to bite my head off for snapping at our mother. To the contrary, they seemed to be concerned about me.

"Are you alright," Dorothy whispered.

"We figured we'd give you some time to cool off after all of the hoopla downstairs," Brandy said, barging into my room, "But when you never came out, we got tired of waiting...What's going on?"

I didn't feel like confiding in my sisters right then. They couldn't relate. Billie had never said much of anything about their fathers. I had often wondered if she even knew who their fathers were.

"She just withheld some very important information from me, that's all."

"That's all?" Brandy replied, "It must've meant a lot to you because you could've awaken the dead the way you were screaming."

"Yeah, we came in on the end. You know, when you told Billie to get to stepping," Dorothy interjected.

I was relieved my sisters had not heard everything I had said. I didn't want to offend them. Funny, I hadn't thought about their feelings when I was venting, but now suddenly that was a major concern.

"Billie has just done a lot to make my life miserable. When she sees me, she sees welcome on my forehead," I said, "This was just the last straw."

Dorothy hugged me again and I already knew what was coming.

"But Ang. You've got to get past whatever it is…we've got to love each other. If we don't who will?"

Suddenly, I realized the irony of Dorothy's favorite philosophy. She was talking about loving each other when for years, she hadn't even loved herself. She had let Glen turn her into a human punching bag. Nevertheless, I knew her comment was heartfelt, so I hugged her back and said, "I know, you're right."

Brandy, then, had to share her point of view. Everybody's a doctor, shoving their opinions down my throat like aspirin. Here's another, no, take this. I had always given them advice, now they were advising me. Still, I felt I did nothing wrong.

"Look, Billie has her ways and I can agree that we are a little messed up because she's such a mess, but the funny thing is that you've never been a mess. It has always amazed me how you run around categorizing yourself with the rest of us. When the fact of the matter is, that you're nothing like us. You never have been and I think you punish yourself because of it. I'm sure whatever she did was pretty bad, but if you're miserable you've got to take some responsibility too."

Ever since Brandy had joined a support group and started going to church, she was always talking about responsibility and account-ability. It must've been part of the group's motto or something. I was so confused. I had one sister telling me I thought I was better than everyone else and now, another telling me I didn't think I was good enough. Anyway, Brandy had no idea what our mother had put me through. Everyone had witnessed her mental abuse but no one had noticed. I've been said to sometimes wear my heart on my sleeve. That must've been the case now, because I could feel that Brandy sensed my outrage regarding her comments. All my life, I had been the responsible one. Shoot, I had been responsible for my life and everyone else's too.

"Look, I'm not saying you shouldn't have told Billie how you feel. Maybe, you should've. I hope it helped. All I'm saying is, no matter what Billie did to set you off, it can't be half as bad as what you've been doing to yourself all this time. If you feel you've been used, you have to remember, no one put a gun to your head and forced you to be a doormat...you volunteered."

CHAPTER 27

THERE'S GOT TO BE MORE THAN THIS

Laquesha was still upset when I got home from work. Billie had left the kids with Jackie earlier in the day while she went to the store. I had told my mother Jackie wasn't allowed in the house anymore but she had never listened to me before so why should she start now? Jackie had told the little girl that she was going to clean her earrings, but as soon as Billie returned, she made a fast getaway with the jewelry. Hours had passed before Laquesha remembered the earrings. Dorothy had been trying to console her ever since. Billie told her Jackie had probably forgotten to give them back, but I believed differently.

"Don't cry baby," I said when I found out what had happened. Hugging her and rocking her back and forth, I said, "I'll buy you some new ones this weekend, some better ones." My niece's tears ceased immediately and she kissed my cheek. I didn't bother saying anything negative about Jackie, especially since I wasn't speaking to Billie anyway. She, too, was giving me the cold shoulder, as though I had somehow slandered her good name. We both knew everything I had said to her was true.

Billie had always hung out downstairs in her "custom built apartment", but now she was constantly upstairs, sitting in the kitchen with the real estate section of the newspaper scattered everywhere-as if she was looking for a place to go.

Brandy had just been hired as the manager of some clothing store in a local strip mall. Dorothy, who was five months pregnant, still was not showing. She had enrolled in Essex County Community College in Newark and even though she was only planning to take three classes, she was proud to be a student. She and I were getting closer each day and I was extremely happy when she asked me to be her coach in the delivery room. I was simply overwhelmed, especially since I had already accepted her offer to be the baby's godmother. Despite Dorothy's accomplishments, she would still get depressed now and then because she couldn't see Glen. I had gone off on her more than once after catching her on the phone with him. Fortunately, I hung up the phone before she had the chance to tell him about the baby. I had advised her to keep it from him until after the birth of the child.

"You shouldn't have to be worried about him right now. You should avoid as much stress as possible and that's all telling him would bring," I had warned.

The sad thing is, that once the child is born, Glen will have a legal right to see him or her. I told Dorothy she shouldn't put his name on the birth certificate -that might prolong the inevitable. I have also begun talking to a real estate agent. I am seriously considering putting the house up for sale. I know that once Glen finds out Dorothy has had his baby, nothing will keep him from coming here. If we move and Dorothy can find enough strength to cease all contact with him, he won't be able to find us. I'll have to make sure Jackie doesn't know our new address either. If she does and he runs into her, she'd probably sell the information for five bucks. I hadn't even shared my latest strategy with Dorothy because I sensed that she was growing weak. "Maybe, he's changed Ang," she mumbled the other day. I didn't argue with my gullible but ever so loving sister. I just reminded her of her past injuries-though they should've been fresh in her mind since she still bore scars-and abandoning all compassion, I reminded her how abruptly her last pregnancy ended. Enough said. I had scared her back to reality.

Everyone's life was changing. I had made some changes as well. Brandy no longer visited the church alone. I accompanied her, most of the time. After my last talk with Brandy, I re-read the scripture Elder Smith had highlighted for me months prior. I needed a foundation. I often felt as though I was a balloon, floating aimlessly, with no anchor in sight. I wanted to be grounded. I needed to believe in something bigger than myself. I needed to believe that everything that I had encountered in my life had purpose. The more I went to church, the better I felt. That peace I had felt while sitting on the patio seemed to be with me much of the time now. It was amazing how much I understood when the preacher taught. I guess, I had indeed, learned a thing or two when I was small. There was a God whose love was so great that he allowed us, his children, to choose our own way. Even if that meant rejection. I had heard it all before, but this time I was listening.

The last time I had gone to church, Elder Smith had told me what a joy it was to see me in the service. When I first saw her from afar, I didn't know whether to run or meet her halfway. She was such a comfort to me, but her insight still frightened me a little. When I think about her words that day, I still smile.

"Baby, I can see you growing spiritually. I see such a change in you, but I know you're still afraid. No need to be. Nothing scary about the Lord's love for you. I know you want to be in control, but the Lord can't drive in the passenger's seat. Don't be afraid to surrender all to him."

I just shook my head in agreement, knowing I had no intention of relinquishing power over my life to anyone. Yet, I felt a battle going on within myself. When I am in church and sometimes when I find myself praying, I feel like I am in another world. I feel an overwhelming urge to just hand everything I have over to God. Then I defiantly force myself back to reality-my reality. I am a strong, independent woman, if nothing else. I, like the rest of my family, have relied on myself for so long that I don't know how to depend on anyone else, and the other part of me doesn't want to give that up in any way.

Daniel had also gone out of his way to acknowledge my presence the last time I went to church. "It's always a pleasure to see you," he had said, grinning. I held my hand out, expecting him to greet me with a handshake as he had done in the past, but instead, he pulled me close and hugged me. There was definitely chemistry, but neither of us had done anything about it and I doubted we ever would. It was better that way. I desperately needed to get my life in order and I didn't need any more distractions...at least, not now.

Now, with that said, you can imagine my shock when I picked up the phone yesterday and heard his voice on the other end. He apologized for not getting my permission before he called but he said he figured it was alright since he had gotten my phone number from my sister. I've always loved her, I said to myself. We talked for hours and it felt like we had known each other our entire lives. He shared stories about his teaching career at St. Paul's Christian Academy. He talked a lot about God and his commitment to him. I didn't doubt his sincerity, yet he was so much more than an avid churchgoer or a musician. I adored his sense of humor and admired his directness. At one point in the conversation, he blurted out,

"I'm thirty-four. I'm not a boy, so I'm not into games. I consider the women and men in my church, family. I don't have any female friends and I'm not looking for any. I am, however, interested in finding someone with whom I can share a loving relationship and my life...I know that sounds serious, but I'm putting all my cards on the table. I want to know if we're on the same page or not because I'd hate to waste your time."

I was completely taken aback, but I managed to respond. Forgetting my vow to avoid distractions, I said, "I'm there". Boy, I never realized honesty was such an attractive attribute. My response-those two words-were the seal of an implied pact. Daniel and I would get to know each other and see if we were as right for each other as we thought we were. He seemed too good to be true but I decided to see where it led.

I was high on life, but my trip didn't last long. Shortly after I hung up with Daniel, Jackie called. Billie must've given her the new number.

"Let me speak to Dorothy," she whispered-without stopping to greet me.

"For what," I snapped.

"None of your business. Just let me...um...talk to her."

Dorothy had told me she had been giving Jackie money. She

said our sister had told her that she was running from some bad people and needed to pay them off quickly. Dorothy didn't even have a job, so she was dipping in a savings account I had started for her and the baby. Once again, Jackie was taking me to the cleaners.

"Jackie, I advise you to get yourself together," I said, "Dorothy doesn't have any more money to give you. You don't need it anyway. What you need is help."

I was left talking to the dial tone. I didn't know what she had gotten herself into, but I knew it wasn't good. She wouldn't be satisfied until she got herself arrested or ended up in some detox unit, or worse. I didn't tell Dorothy she called. She was already worried sick about her and I didn't want to get her anymore upset. After all, I had to look out for my godchild. Instead, I shared the news about Daniel. She was happier than I was.

"Oh, I hope everything works out for you Ang. He sounds great," she said, "You deserve more than anyone, to be happy. I was starting to get worried. You've been by yourself for way too long."

"Yeah, too long," I echoed.

CHAPTER 28

SHADES OF BLACK

I must've had the gift of prophecy, I thought, as I pulled up to my house. A police car was parked in front. What had Jackie done now and why were the cops at my house? Knowing her, she had probably used my name or my address when she did whatever horrible thing she had done.

When I entered the home, I knew I couldn't be more wrong. A darkness seemed to loom over the foyer. It was apparent that something far worse had taken place as I saw two officers holding Billie upright. I left my body at that moment. I saw everything that was happening. I could hear one of the officers calling to me, "Miss... Miss...are you alright?" and I could hear Billie wailing, "No, no, not my baby, not my baby."

It was a dark, rainy day-a perfect day for a funeral. All of Dorothy's former peers and friends paid their respect. There had to be a closed casket because the force of the bullet had blown away half her skull. I think it was easier to say goodbye to her that way. I don't think I could've just walked away if I had been able to see her beautiful face, full of innocence, laying there as if in a peaceful sleep. Yes, it had been easier to look upon the black box-pretending for a moment, that it was empty; that the entire tragedy had been nothing but a nightmare.

The past three days, I had gone over the story a hundred times in my head. Dorothy had rushed out of the house after answering the phone, according to Billie. My mother said she thought nothing of it. Somehow, Dorothy had ended up at Glen's apartment. He had taken the day off from work-he obviously had a plan. Nana was one of the first to hear the gunshots. Fearing the worse, she banged on the door and when no one answered, she dialed 911. By the time the police arrived, there was a crowd in the hallway of the building. They knocked the door down and discovered Dorothy and Glen's bodies. Nana told the officers where they could find her family so they could notify us.

We assume, now, that it had been Glen who called Dorothy that day. No one knows what he said to entice her to the apartment. Had he found out about the baby? Had he threatened to take his own life? No one knows. The only thing that was certain was the fact that three people were dead-my sister, her boyfriend and their child. I had tried, but I couldn't protect them. I had failed. I kept thinking, maybe if I hadn't urged Dorothy to go back to school, she'd be alive today. Maybe I had caused her to miss Glen by telling her about my conversations with Daniel. To punish myself, I avoided him altogether-refusing all of his phone calls.

I looked at the program one more time before sticking it into my bible. On the front of it, there was a photo of Dorothy smiling. Gazing at the picture, you'd never know her life had been filled with such pain. At the bottom of the page, her name was next to the timeline 1976-1998 and the words, "A Special Lady Indeed."

Brandy, Gina, Billie, the kids and I sat on the front pew of the church, dressed in shades of black. Pastor Ellis and the Greater Love congregation had been nice enough to offer us the use of the church for the funeral, even though Dorothy was not a member. Brandy had recently joined and the pastor said any family of hers was family of theirs. Two empty spaces were next to us. Jackie hadn't showed up and I had not been able to get in touch with Rosa-she was on vacation with her family. I had left several messages on her voicemail and she had yet to return any. As I looked around the church, there were several people I didn't recognize. They were church members who had come to the funeral to offer their prayers and support. Daniel was among them. He came over to where I was sitting, kissed me on my cheek and whispered, "I'm here if you need me." Then he walked away as quickly as he had approached.

Just as the service was ending, I walked to the podium to read the poem I had written in Dorothy's honor.

> So loving and so demure
> Her conscience was so pure
> Seeing the world as sisters and brothers
> She challenged us all to love one another
> She knew hate destroys and apathy kills
> If we don't love each other, then, who will?
> A daughter, a sister, a compassionate friend
> A mother, a beauty, outside and in
> She touched the lives of all she knew
> Sincerity and love inspired all she'd do
> She'd let you in her life and her heart was open widely
> Dorothy was a rare jewel... a special lady indeed

I dropped Gina, Laquesha, Tonya and Wadell off at my house after the funeral. I told them I had to run a quick errand and I'd be back soon. Before my sister could ask any questions, I sped off. I needed to be alone. I needed to go somewhere and think. I started to return to my favorite spot-South Mountain Reservation, but I quickly found myself traveling in the opposite direction. As I drove past teenage hoodlums, liquor stores and barber shops, I couldn't help but ponder on the transformation my old neighborhood had undergone. The streets looked drastically different than they had when Rosa and I had lived here with Grandma Helen and Grandpa George. As I turned down my old street, I said softly, "The homes are still beautiful." I don't know why I had chosen to come here. Maybe, because my grandparents had always been a source of great strength for me and this was the only tangible reminder left of them. It was still on the market, so far Aunt Lizzy hadn't been successful in finding a buyer. I needed to be strong now more than ever. With the car still running, I glanced over every section of the house. As I reflected on all the wonderful memories I had shared in the home, a peace came over me. I hadn't even noticed the man standing on the lawn holding a newspaper, until now. He was staring at the house too. As our eyes met, I couldn't help but feel as though I knew him. Something about his face made me want to draw closer, but glancing at the clock on the dashboard, I realized it was getting late. I'd better head home.

Church members had been bringing dishes by my house daily. Today, as I shuffled into the house, past the for sale sign, the smell of pastries and tuna casserole tickled my nose. I joined everyone, all of whom seemed to be gazing into space, and took my place around the kitchen table. Even the children were quiet, with the exception of little Tonya. She'd let out a coo every now and then. The others had been traumatized by the loss of someone so precious. I sent them downstairs to watch television. The doorbell rang and Brandy went to answer it. She re-entered the kitchen with Jackie. She had lost about fifteen pounds and looked as though she had just fallen out of bed, not the glamorous sibling we were accustomed to seeing. "I'm so sorry Billie," she said, kissing our mother on the cheek, but Billie didn't say a word. She just sat there staring at the program. I wanted to ask Jackie where she had been. What had been so important that she had missed her baby sister's funeral? But I remained quiet. She hadn't been there for Dorothy when she was alive, she might as well not be there for her in death.

I walked over to the radio on the corner of the countertop and flicked the on switch. Sam Cooks' soulful voice filled the room as he sang, "I don't want to live, but I'm too afraid to die. It's been a long time coming, but I know, a change goin' come, a change goin' come."

We all had been through so much in our lifetimes-we had witnessed so much for so long. I had spent my life trying to be everything to everybody and I had lost myself in the process. Now, Dorothy was dead. A change had to come. This family couldn't stay the same. The singer had summed it up in a melody. I broke the silence and began to sing along. "A change goin' come, a change goin' come." Everyone's eyes shifted toward me like I had performed a sacrilegious act. I closed my eyes and began to sing louder. Soon, Brandy tuned in, then Gina. Jackie looked bewildered. Billie screamed, "Shut up, shut up," but we continued to harmonize. Dorothy's death had been the final wake up call to the

Roberts family. Realizing that resistance would prove to be futile, Billie grew quiet once again, as we continued-unified, sharing our victory song.

That night I knelt down beside my bed as had become my nightly ritual before Dorothy's death. I hadn't prayed since. I was angry, just as I had been when I was a little girl. I wanted to know why. Why did Dorothy have to die? Now, after some soul searching, I realized it wasn't God's fault. God hadn't advised Dorothy to hook up with Glen. He hadn't led her to his apartment. He hadn't put the gun in his hand, and neither had I. I couldn't control my family. I didn't have that kind of power. Ms. Tower of Strength-Pinnacle of Independence...I couldn't even control my own life. So, I closed my eyes tightly and as the tears fell, my heart melted and I said-certainty in my voice-"I surrender Lord, I surrender. Please, Jesus," I pleaded, "Come into my heart. Forgive all of my sins and cleanse me. I invite you to be my Savior and Lord. Please, take control. I want Your will to be done in my life. I've lived for my family. Now, I want to live for you."

CHAPTER 29

EVERYTHING MUST CHANGE

"Where is my other shoe," I said aloud, as I searched every room in the two- bedroom condo I now called home. I didn't want to be late for church. I was supposed to pick Brandy up ten minutes ago.

After Dorothy died, I saw no reason not to go through with my original plans and sell the house. I was blessed enough to find a two story condominium in my price range, which meant I wouldn't have to worry about lawn care, snow removal…nothing. I wouldn't have time to maintain a home anyway since I had replaced Dorothy at the nursing home and the youth center. It had been nine months since her death and they were missing her almost as much as I was. I had also volunteered to spend some of my Saturday mornings helping out at Safe Haven - a shelter for battered women and their children.

Remembering the serenity of my old patio, I made sure I bought a unit with a balcony, so I could exhale every now and then. "Found it," I exclaimed, when I saw the burgundy and black snake skin pump peeking from underneath the sofa. I must've left it there when I kicked it off the other day after work. The condo was empty and I could hear my voice slightly echo as the sound waves bounced off of the cathedral ceilings. As I grabbed my keys off the living room table and headed toward the front door, I couldn't help but reflect. There would be no children screaming my name when I returned, no music blasting, no fussing or fighting. I was still getting used to living alone. It was a liberating, yet a peculiar transition to make.

My niece and nephews were now living with Gina. She had moved into a slightly bigger apartment, after getting a job as a receptionist at a beauty salon. She was still receiving some financial assistance, but I was proud of the steps she was taking toward independence. I still saw the kids. Some Sundays I'd bring them to church with me and I made sure I set aside at least one Saturday afternoon a month to take them somewhere. Billie had also moved in with my sister, of course the Department of Welfare didn't know that. They would've cut Gina off completely if they knew another fully-abled adult was living with her. With Billie staying there, Gina didn't have to pay for child care. The truth is, Billie needed those kids just as much as they needed her.

No one has heard from Jackie, but the rumor is, that she is frequently seen on Nye Avenue in Newark - an infamous hooker hangout. Brandy and I had spent weeks driving up and down the road trying to find her. Sometimes we still drive down the street, hoping to get a glimpse of her so we can offer our help. The truth be told, we are actually relieved each time we go and don't see her. We don't want the rumors to be true, even though we know they probably are.

Church was packed as usual, but Brandy and I managed to find seats in one of the pews toward the back of the church. Daniel winked at me as I sat down-flashing that trademark smile. My man was fine indeed.

Toward the end of the service, I turned around to look at the clock, which was awkwardly hung on the back wall of the sanctuary. As I did, someone in the last pew caught my eye. She was dressed in a royal blue mini skirt with a matching jacket that had black beaded buttons down the front. I recognized the outfit as one Billie had come home with, after exchanging the conservative black Liz Claiborne suit I had purchased for her as a birthday gift. Her face bore no emotion as she sat there looking straight ahead. How had Billie gotten here? Why had she even come? Even with those questions running through my mind, I couldn't help but smile as I nudged my sister. "As long as there's life in the body, there's hope," I whispered, as I shifted my eyes toward our mother, hinting for Brandy to turn around. She turned around and her mouth hung open in shock as she returned to her forward position.

Billie didn't seem to be enjoying herself, but at least she had come. The choir came forth to render a closing selection. I turned around again. I could see my mother's mouth begin to move a little as she attempted to discreetly join the congregation in song. My heart leapt, and I mumbled like grandma used to, "Who wouldn't serve a God like this?"

Are *You* Ready For A Change?

If you have tried to make something out of your life but realize now that only the Creator of life can do that, surrender as Angela did. If you are sick and tired of being sick and tired and, like Angela, want to experience the peace of God in your life, pray with me now:

> Lord, please come into my heart and live there. I accept you as my personal Savior and Lord. I believe you died on the cross for the forgiveness of my sins. I believe you did not stay dead, but rose with all power in Your hand. I renounce the devil and every one of his works in my life. Cleanse me Jesus and Lord, take control of Me. I am Yours now and from this moment forward, I will walk in newness of life. I am a new person, Thank You Jesus!
>
> In Jesus' Name, Amen

I praise God for you and I know you will never be the same again! Now, I encourage you to find a good church where you can learn more about your Savior, Jesus Christ. Listen to the Word of God on t.v., on radio, on tapes, cds, etc.. For this will increase your faith and teach you how to live a life that's pleasing in God's sight. Lastly, talk to God just like you'd talk to a friend. There is no formula to prayer. Talk to Him honestly and talk to Him often! I pray that you will fall in love with the Lord just as I have and that you will remain faithful to Him always. God bless!

To Book This Author for Speaking Engagements or Book Signings, please send requests to:

Terri Jones Salter
1075 Easton Avenue, #203
Somerset, New Jersey 08873
or simply visit www.sinsofmymother.com